Love Tarot For Beginners

Romantic Interpretations for Every Card In the Tarot Deck

Jhone Daniels

Dedicated to Eric

The King of My Particular Everything

Table of Contents

INTRODUCTION

Tarot is fascinating and fun. I find it captivating enough to have kept at it for nearly thirty years. What I've learned during that time is that most folks want answers to questions about love, romance, and sex.

Of course, you care about your job or the occasional specific issue, but by and large people want answers to questions such as "Does he/she love me?" "Is he/she the right one for me?" "What's going to happen now?" and the daunting, "Why are they doing... *that*?"

This book will open the veil! If you have tried to read Tarot, you may have come to the conclusion that only about a third of the cards concern themselves with relationships and emotions. In truth, if you know how to look, all of the cards of the Tarot deck have meanings that fall into the Big Three of Inquiry: Love, Money, and Work.

Rare indeed is the book defining Tarot cards which focuses in a detailed manner on the LOVE aspect of a reading, but that's what we are going for here! Even a true novice will be able to do a love spread and understand what each card means vis-à-vis romance. Impress your friends! Dazzle your enemies! Win the heart of The Queen of Cups!

This book jumps right to it, and while I do provide a short and basic traditional definition before jumping into the Good Stuff, this handy guide is all you need to finally KNOW what to think about that pesky Two of Swords and the other ambivalent cards.

I am assuming here that you have a spread or two you like, and a technique of shuffling that works for you. I have included some especially helpful and classic spreads at the end of the book, but my focus with this guide is simply to give you a romantic interpretation for every card in the deck.

I also include an "Outcome Card" context, which can be the most confusing aspect of a spread, but remember: *ALL cards relate to each other*. A thrilling spread with a lousy outcome card doesn't mean all is lost. It just means: "Be careful and smart." Know that the best way to read Tarot is to tell a story with it; each card is a chapter, flowing into the next. With practice, you will become so fluent in this language you will see the story unfold in front of you, and when it comes to love and divination, you will have a real leg up. But, before we begin, a little background.

HOW DOES TAROT WORK?

OR:

HOW TO MAKE YOUR CARDS CRANKY

When new to Tarot I assigned some qualities to it that I have come to modify with time, experience, and thousands of readings. In fact, it was many years before I truly came to understand what I believe is the real "magic" of tarot.

There is a lot of lore surrounding the cards, and it is difficult to know Tarot's true origin, but the first cards found using the symbols that eventually became the Major Arcana were in a five hundred year old card game called "Trumps" (ahem). Seeing some one's future in cards, tea leafs or entrails is a long standing human tradition, but I often wonder who was the first person to try!

So, while there is no true consensus as to How it All Got Started, it is probably satisfyingly simple and practical, like all human beginnings, and then coated in many dips of mythic embellishment over time, because that is one of the things humans do best: We make things important by all choosing to agree they are important, and then add a dose of time for gravitas. The amazing part about this is this often works! This imaginary important thing becomes real, and really works. That is a type of true magic.

Tarot is the Velveteen Rabbit of divination, and for this useful tool, I am very grateful.

Now that we are on the subject of divination, I should add here that Tarot does not tell you the future in a "set in stone" way, at all. Your reading is a bummer? Well, that's OK, because what Tarot does is give you a snapshot of your current state, and then suggests that, given the current circumstances, and only if you do nothing to change them, there is a likelihood of the following happening. The future is very fluid, and it is extremely rare that Tarot predicts something that is completely out of your hands to change. Yes, there are exceptions. When the Tower shows up…something is coming down, and you are going to be a spectator in that experience, and soon, but this is rare.

So how does it work? I have a theory, and it is very Jungian at its core. Carl Jung (super-genius, and one of the founders of the general umbrella under which we tuck the practice of psychoanalysis, as well as a true mystic), brought forth the idea of the Collective Unconsciousness…and to wildly simplify that concept, it is the idea that the whole of human experience, the entire planet and every human and other being on it is a part of a larger energetic entity: the collective experience of the species Human.

This is an energy and influence of its own, separate from your own unconscious, and the cards, with their archetypal ideas (archetypes being fundamental human concepts found across all cultures: sun, moon, mother, father, love, death, renewal, hope, etc)…tap into that energy and express it by showing you where you are going in the Big Blue Experience of Life on Earth.

Or, if that is too woo, you can think of the cards as a nice way to make you think; it is a symbolic kick in the pants to get you unstuck, or see things from another perspective.

Either works. In fact, they are so uncannily accurate most of the time that belief in them in order for them to work is entirely unnecessary. I cannot tell you how many readings I have done with someone who started out with crossed arms and an incredulous expression, and ended with open palms and a sense of wonder.

In the end, it's important to realize that the cards are simply a helpful tool that can keep you aware, focused and creative with regards to problems, but you need never feel helpless to their presented outcome. You have all the power here, and this is just a window to help you see clearly.

And this brings up an important point! You don't need to read about the same question over and over and over and over. That way lies madness, Star Pirate. Use the following definitions and spreads to see possibilities, and then let it go until there is a new development. You can then read again, with the blessing of the cards, so to speak.

If you read compulsively, which I know is very, very tempting when you are upset or very attached to someone and want to know what will happen next, your answer will get muddier and muddier, and there is no comfort in that. The cards can even become tricksters after a while, giving you complete gobbledygook or hilariously awful, impossibly bad readings.

We can't have that, right? So respect the cards and they will respect you by giving you clear, accurate readings that excite, comfort and even warn of impending drama...drama you can usually avoid, if you are smart. (P.S: You are so smart!)

Turn to the chapters after the definitions for some of my favorite spreads, how to read them, and example readings.

ON "REVERSED CARDS"

While there is a tradition that says it is "proper" to read cards that land upside down (or "reversed") with their accompanying near opposite meaning, I'm saying it isn't, and I am not alone. There is no "rule" that says you have to do this, and frankly, if you are aware of the darker aspects of any card, then that's really all you need.

Just go with me on this. The Tarot deck is a beautiful mix of positive and… less positive. They are perfect as they are, with both light and dark aspects built into each card. Why literally stack these cards against you?

I read upright only. Life is complicated enough.

Bonne Chance!
Jhone

THE MAJOR ARCANA

Image copyright J. Daniels with elements used with permission.

These are the Big Baddies. The Archetypes. The Human Experience across all cultures! Therefore, the meanings will be richer than the simpler and more everyday experiences of the four suits.

Tarot spreads that fall with a majority of Major Arcana cards within them are considered to be "fateful," or out of your hands.

You are far too smart, wise, and attractive to believe that.

If you draw a spread that is made up of mostly Major Arcana cards, then it makes sense to consider the spread rather important. Still, you should never let that stop you from wrestling your destiny to the ground, tying it up prettily, and making it your own. We might not get to have everything we want, but we certainly don't have to be passive about it. Don't like an outcome? Change it. You are a clever thing. Captain your Ship of Destiny like the swashbuckling star pirate we both know you are. I have faith in you.

Let's go!

0: THE FOOL

TRADITIONAL MEANING

Faith, chance-taking, foolishness, and things that work out in spite of lack of savvy. Risking all. Fearlessness. Spiritual Journey.

LOVE READING

Oh, The Fool. If he is the Querent (the question asker): his heart is sewn to his sleeve with the reddest of threads! His utter willingness to throw himself into love without being mindful of the possible painful consequences is the stuff of romantic legend! Conversely, maybe you are blind to the faults of your paramour? Maybe you have a crush on an appealing and quirky character that falls somewhere between eccentric artist and goofily appealing man-child (or ageless manic pixie)? This lover will be unlike your usual fare, and he or she might baffle and frustrate, as well as excite you, if you are the rescuing type (don't be the rescuing type).

It's likely that they are great fun, and very inventive in the sack, while also scattered and a bit disorganized in their life, and yes, a bit immature. Still, fun; that is until you realize you might slowly be turning into "Mom."

Watch out if The Fool is paired with The Devil, as this can suggest addiction, or The Magician, as this can suggest that The Fool's innocent exterior hides a clever con artist.

If this card appears in a reading with The Five of Pentacles or The Emperor, watch out for a "bad boy" addiction. Trying to win the heart of the unwinnable will only bring you heartache.

As a situation, it can mean complete and utter faith on the part of the Querent that "things are being handled" by the Universe. Sometimes it's a very good thing to just let go and have faith in best outcomes, if only because it allows the Beloved to come to you, rather than chasing after someone. (That's also the job of The Hanged Man, whom we will visit shortly.)

POSSIBLE OUTCOME

Whoo, boy. Nothing is certain or settled here. Keep a positive attitude, pay attention, and make sure you are not letting your deeply romantic heart blind yourself to a bouquet of red flags being thrust in your face. In an otherwise very positive spread, see this card as a sign to back off a bit… to let go and let them come forward and do a bit of the heavy lifting for a bit. This is a dance for you both to enjoy, rather than a forced march!

1: THE MAGICIAN

TRADITIONAL MEANING

Manifestation of desires. Magic. Power and control. Creating something from nothing. The Trickster.

LOVE READING

Hm. I don't know about this guy. He's a bit of a smoothie, this one. A bit polished. This is a man who always says all the right things. You know who always says all the right things? Someone with a whole lot of practice! This is the card of the Pickup Artist Community.

Sure. He or she might actually BE an impossibly attractive, hugely articulate, confident, financially smart, funny as hell SEX GOD. Sure. They exist! Why shouldn't one fall into your lap? He might also be all those things and a little concerned, say, about the true nature of his sexual orientation, and would like to use you as an experiment while he works that one out.

Or maybe "I'm in banking" actually means "I'm a teller at a bank", and while there is nothing wrong with that honorable occupation, because this is the card of the embellisher, watch out. Some people just don't feel truly lovable unless they make themselves seem very special. If you are willing to wade through that and get to their insecure, possibly loveable core, you might find a person of real quality there. Or, you might be off to the therapist for years! Only time will tell. Whee! Careful, lover!

As a situation and NOT a person, The Magician is a Very Different Animal. In this case, it is your ability to make things work and manifest in spite of obstacles. It's about creating magic in your life, because you simply won't accept anything else. It's about creating a meal out of a near empty fridge to hold the both of you over till a time when you are better off, and this is great. Just know that you can't drink from an empty cup forever.

POSSIBLE OUTCOME

In this position, it is most likely a situation, rather than a person, and that outcome is positive. This is snatching victory from the jaws of defeat. Savor it.

2: THE HIGH PRIESTESS

TRADITIONAL MEANING

Mystery. Feminine power. Magic. Chastity. An emotionally removed woman. Esoteric knowledge.

LOVE READING

Playing it cool, are we? Playing a bit hard to get? You or your interest are holding your cards tightly to your chest, and you have no idea where you stand, or are working hard to keep them guessing! It works, actually, and someone will be eating out of someone else's hand soon, but you can't keep up this icy persona forever, nor can you subject yourself to it indefinitely. True emotional intimacy means getting messy, revealing your vulnerabilities, and indulging in the occasional ugly cry.

This is also the card of the Inappropriate Crush. Your boss, your professor, your friend's spouse, oh my! So many opportunities for you to be miserably unfulfilled! Maybe the inappropriateness of the crush is simply more about wanting someone to be more than they can be, emotional-availability wise. Sometimes we go for Mr. or Ms. Chill when we fear intimacy ourselves. If the object of our adoration is an emotional wall, then we are free to fling ourselves against it in delicious passion and longing without ever having to deal with the complete terror of having your love actually being returned in full measure. If you had a crush on Spock, then this dynamic might be your jam. This is a theme that will come up more than once in this book, as it's a classic human experience.

One final possibility: looks like sex might not be a priority in this relationship, or what was once very passionate has cooled quite a bit. Before you accuse a partner of not having a high enough libido, pay very close attention to your own behavior as a lover. Always, but *always*, seek to examine your own behavior first before moving on to blame.

POSSIBLE OUTCOME

Ah. This is a card of “Stop. Go No Further.” Bummer. When this Mysterious Lady lands in the outcome position, it means that all will not yet be revealed. Sigh. This is NOT the time to keep asking the same question, shuffling and reading and shuffling and reading and shuffling and reading and shuffling and reading and… well, you know this sad and hopeful dance I’m leading here. Not to worry. This is temporary. When you sense movement in the situation, you can pick up those cards again.

3: THE EMPRESS

TRADITIONAL MEANING
Luxury. Opulence. Fertility. Femininity. Romance. Marriage. Home and garden.

LOVE READING
Whenever this regal and lux woman shows up in a spread, I inevitably think the same thing: "Hello, Bouncy!"

I can't help it. The Empress is supposed to be an elegant creature, and she is, but she can also be a bit unaware and clueless, too, as she is used to being taken care of to such a degree that she no longer understands how the rest of us struggle to live. Bubbly and kind and sweet to a fault, this hostess with the mostest is a great deal of fun. However, don't mistake what seems like wide-eyed innocence for stupidity. She is anything but. She is just *pure of intent* in a world of cynicism.

But why "Bouncy?" Because this woman is all woman: very feminine, voluptuous, flirty, sexy, and, if you aren't careful… fertile. This means she is great news if you are looking to become pregnant.

But for the rest of us who aren't, no need to get nervous. She can also mean traditional romance, as in that frisson that comes with the polar dynamic of male and female gender roles, romantically rather than oppressively expressed. This is doubly true if The Emperor shows up in the same spread. Also, it can be about money and luxury itself, as in having the means to enjoy yourself completely with your partner: to go where you want, do what you want, and the time and freedom to do so. Also, lots and lots and lots of sex! Yay, sex!

If there is a downside to this sweetheart, it's that she might have an overdeveloped sense of entitlement of which she is completely unaware, simply because she is used to living a very comfortable life. Still, she is a very good hearted, generous soul, indeed. If your crush is this woman, traditionally a blond or a redhead, then go for it. She will be an excellent companion, lover, and muse. Just be sure to treat her to little luxuries as you can, or at least overlook her own small indulgences. If you are the woman in question, enjoy and play up your most feminine aspects, as they will be highly valued by your romantic interest.

POSSIBLE OUTCOME

Nice! This is one of the small groups of cards that tend to mean "And they lived happily ever after!" Look for these other cards to show up in the reading to confirm this: The Lovers, The Hierophant, The Sun, The Star, The Nine of Cups, The Two of Cups, Aces of Wands or Cups, and any of The King cards of any suit. In answer to "Will I have children?", this card in the outcome position is considered the strongest indicator of "Yes!" in the deck.

4: THE EMPEROR

TRADITIONAL MEANING

Traditional Masculinity. Leadership. Oppression. Rigidity. Power. Overwhelming force. Conservative.

LOVE READING

Most of the time, The Emperor is a person in your life of great importance or influence to you at the time of the reading. This can be a good thing. This can be a neutral thing, if you get my meaning. This card can just represent The Man in Question, and nothing more, except signaling that he is important to you!

On the other hand, if you are reading about character traits, and wondering what kind of person you are dealing with, then I should give you both the good and the… less than good!

The Good

If you like traditionally masculine, protective men, well, it's your lucky day! The Emperor is an excellent provider, often a leader in the community or his career, and oh, boy, would your mom approve. MANLY.

The Less Than Good

Did I mention manly? Well, it's not *cute, funny, and charming Nick Offerman* manly. It's usually the *"I wash my hair with dish soap because shampoo is for girls"* manly. It's *"I call women 'gals' or 'females', and wow, they are sweet, but irrational. Am I right?"* manly, and that sort of masculinity can be a bit fragile. Brittle. Rigid. Conservative. At its core, it's an insecure and precarious image to maintain.

Sure, he's an excellent protector and provider, if you are someone who needs a lot of protection and provision, but your tears make him either angry or confused, and this kind of "protection" sometimes comes with a price, whether it's something "small," like resentment, or something large, like oppressive abuse.

In his more benign aspects, when you have a problem of any kind, he is sure he can solve it with graph paper and a pencil. His natural leadership abilities can get twisted up in the wrong hands and become his natural *"Let's oppress everyone to make sure I get my way"* abilities. There are a lot of little Emperors in the world. Some of them even run for President.

Be particularly careful if this card shows up in a spread with The Five of Pentacles. This suggests a strong attraction to "bad boy" types who talk a very good game, but are really unavailable emotionally. They might look great on paper, but words are not deeds, and rare is it that the words and deeds of this combination match.

So, if you dig this guy, let's hope he is that magic blend of traditional Knightly Protector and Sensitive Lover. He exists, but he's a bit of a Manicorn, so good luck to you!

If it is clear that this is not a person, and merely a situation, then you can read it like this: you will be dealing with a steamroller of a situation. Get ready to resist, evade, or submit.

POSSIBLE OUTCOME

Back to the beginning. A man who is currently insignificant in your life will greatly increase in importance to you.

5: THE HIEROPHANT

TRADITIONAL MEANING

Tradition itself. The Church. Authority. Council. Commitment. Marriage. Becoming an acolyte.

LOVE READING

The Hierophant is an interesting card in that it is greatly affected by the cards that are also in the spread. In this way it is much like pasta! If it is in a spread with many favorable romance cards, then it very often signals not only commitment, but a possibility of living together or even an engagement. This card paired with The Lovers, The Two of Cups, The Three of Cups, or any Knight or King (or Empress or Queen!) pumps up the juju on that being the likely future.

In the absence of these or a reading with many ill-favored cards, it can instead suggest the opposite: a desire to retreat a bit, focus on your traditional pursuits, and spend time with platonic friends.

It also can suggest a time of actual retreat! Going to meditate and drink cleansing juices for a week? This would be the card that suggests now is a good time for that and coming back renewed for a fresh start.

POSSIBLE OUTCOME

As an outcome card in a favorable spread, a happy commitment is definitely in the cards. In an unfavorable spread, this one might peter out simply because outside pressures of conformity, and possible religious incompatibility, are too great to overcome.

6: THE LOVERS

TRADTIONAL MEANING

Love. Passion. Sex. Choice. Soul mate. Temptation. Desire. Lust.

LOVE READING

Okay, now we're Taroting with gas! In a relationship spread, The Lovers card is, of course, unambiguously about love and all the goodies that come with. So, this meaning is very straightforward and does not alter much from a traditional definition. In other types of spreads, it can simply mean "a difficult choice, filled with temptation," but here it's all romance. Not insubstantial romance either, or the casual, playful, light romance of The Six of Cups, for example. This is hot and heady stuff, fraught with passion and possibly life-altering choices.

Certain cards strongly affect how and in what way the Lovers will express themselves:

Paired with The Star

You might be a bit blind to the faults of your new love, but not in a negative way. Hold on to that blindness for as long as you can, as in that way lies peace! Flirt with abandon! Go for it! This is a yes if both of these cards are in a spread.

Paired with The Sun

JACKPOT, baby! Let hope reign supreme, but with its best and most sought after companion, FULFILLMENT. This is Happily Ever After time, and one of the most positive and sought after card combinations in Tarot!

Paired with The Devil

With most cards being positive, oh, my! You two are kinksters! Sexual astronauts! Enjoy your well-matched kink!

Paired with Negative Cards
Watch your tendency to become a bit obsessive and overindulgent. Don't gobble each other up all at once, lest this burn hot and heavy, and then quickly sputter out in a pool of tequila, stale donuts, handcuffs, and sweaty regret. Also, watch out for issues of addiction!

Paired with The Seven of Swords
Temptation and possible infidelity, but of the shallow and selfish sort rather than Soulmate Lightning. Temporary pleasures taken that risk long-term pain. Watch out. Don't ruin a good thing; think carefully before making a life altering choice!

Paired with The Nine of Cups
LOVE WISH FULLFILLED! ACHIEVEMENT UNLOCKED!

Paired with the Two of Cups
You lucky dog. This is considered the most romantic of combinations in Tarot. If there is such a thing as a sure thing, you have drawn it. Enjoy.

POSSIBLE OUTCOME

Hold on to your knickers! You are in for a fun time! Don't blow it! Be present; don't live in the future. Pay attention to how this romance makes YOU feel, rather than how much you want the other person to like you.

7: THE CHARIOT

TRADITIONAL MEANING

Triumph through might. Strong willpower. Good self control, culminating in victory. Making a choice.

LOVE READING

Whoo. You really want this bad. You want it so bad you are somewhat willing to ride a bit roughshod over the feelings of others. There is a chance here that you might think that will sheer force of will you can make your desired outcome happen, but remember, lover, there are two in this tango.

Another, less aggressive interpretation is one of choice. A case where this card might show up in a love spread is under the dilemma of knowing that you have two strong options for love in front of you and knowing that it will soon be time to choose one. This can mean literally two people, or it can mean two lifestyles, such as "Do you stay uncommitted with the potential fun of having all options open to you, or do you take the plunge, commit, and reap the benefits of happy coupledom?"

Just remember, either way, The Chariot is a card of might and self-interest, and those are two things that need to be used very carefully in romance. A light touch works best!

POSSIBLE OUTCOME

You win! Be a good winner, and remember that others' feelings matter just as well as your own.

8: STRENGTH

TRADITIONAL MEANING

Gentle force applied with skill. Strong character. The ability to master your impulsiveness and be effective in the world.

LOVE READING

The lover that possesses the characteristics of the Strength card is a wonderful partner indeed. As a person or a situation, the traits of calm, self-restraint, wisdom, kindness, strong moral character, gentleness, perseverance, patience, maturity, and attractiveness prevail.

The man who is represented by the Strength card is a dreamboat; the woman, a gentle, wise, sexy, confident and intelligent paramour.

This is the card of the grown-up. Possessed of high levels of emotional intelligence, this card represents someone you can introduce to friends and family with pride. This is someone who doesn't run at the first sign of trouble; is gentle, but firm in their feeling; has learned from hard-won experience; and is no pushover. Gentle confidence is the order of the day.

Don't mistake this for dull, and, if you *do*, carefully examine your own issues with intimacy. For some of us, when it comes to our love lives, the only thing that feels right is conflict, and the only thing that feels normal is feeling bad or confused or unsure. Sometimes fear of intimacy doesn't show up as running away from someone, but running toward the wrong someone. That way, you can have the passionate experience of intense desire, longing, and "love" without ever having to worry about the terror of having this love actually returned.

As an experience, it means everyone involved is sane, kind, warm, and wanting the best outcome for all concerned.

This card boosts the good qualities of the positive cards it is near, and softens the dark aspects of the negative.

It's a great card to have show up in a love spread.

POSSIBLE OUTCOME

Everyone is going to play nice, *or* you will have the self-control, the maturity, to do the right thing, in the right way, and handle it like a boss.

9: THE HERMIT

TRADTIONAL MEANING

Meditation. Time alone. Finding a mentor. Intense study. Arcane knowledge.

LOVE READING

Well, there is no getting around it: The Hermit is not the very best card to show up in a reading, but where it lands, and what is near, impacts the meaning of the card a great deal.

In the past positions of a spread, it can speak of loneliness, or a desire to withdraw and focus on learning, personal interests, or education. Having this card show up in a past position can often mean this time of aloneness is about to end!

In the future positions, though, it can quite strongly suggest a breakup, especially when paired with traditional romance cards like The Lovers, The Two of Cups, The Nine of Cups, The Empress, etc. It is the archetypal rejection of intimate connection with others, emotional unavailability, and emotional withdrawal. It also can mean that you have fallen for someone who is emotionally very distant, or of an anxious/avoidant attachment style. This means that they are quickly overwhelmed by too much intimacy, or find it very difficult to access their emotions and express them. These people need love, too, and often seek it out, but sometimes they create pain and confusion for their partners, who are a bit starved for attention, and frustrated that their Hermit lover doesn't seem to understand what they need emotionally.

Here is the good side to the breakup that results from this card: it's good to know when something isn't working. It's *very* brave to say it out loud and make a change. Many couples, not happy, and not well suited, stay together long after they should have let their relationship go, because they fear change, fear loss, or sometimes, simply fear stating the truth! When a relationship isn't working, it's important to fix what you can, or realize what isn't fixable, and move on, so you both have a chance at finding happiness elsewhere. Someone brave enough to step up and gently end the unworkable is a good person, and this ending can be a gift!

POSSIBLE OUTCOME

It looks like you will be uncoupled for now, but now is not forever! Take good care of yourself while you have this time alone. Do fun things! Learn a new skill! Rediscover yesteryear's forgotten glory of Air Supply! Remember those hobbies you abandoned when you fell in love? DO THEM!!! Also, quit abandoning hobbies when you fall in love!

10: THE WHEEL OF FORTUNE

TRADITIONAL MEANING

Change of luck, change in fortune. Usually positive.

LOVE READING

Good times are on their way! At least they are if they aren't so flipping good right now. The most profound and basic meaning of The Wheel is that "this too shall pass," and this applies to love spreads as well.

When this card shows up in a romance spread, it tends to mean that a shift in attitude or circumstance is about to happen, and most likely it will be a welcome and lucky change! This is not a powerful or deep card, though, when it comes to relationships. It's more of a simple reminder that the road to love is never a straight path, and there will be twists and turns.

Having said that, these twists are usually good ones, when this friendly card shows up. Look for lucky circumstances to gently shift the tone of your romance toward a more lighthearted and pleasurable time.

POSSIBLE OUTCOME

This is a lucky card in the outcome position. It tends to be of the "wish granted" variety, but don't rest on your laurels here. This is a card of change, most of all, and remembering there is no constant and learning to go with the flow is important.

11: JUSTICE

TRADITIONAL MEANING

Legal issues. Winning. Issues of fairness. Equality.

LOVE READING

Justice, I admit, is not a sexy card. It often has to do with legal issues, which, in a love spread, can mean divorce, custody issues, and other super fun stuff. Bad news? You are in court. Good news? Looks like you win.

More subtly though, there are, in fact, interesting aspects to this card, as well, and they are important in a love spread! For example, having the Justice card show up, with its scales and measures, could mean that there are issues of balance in your relationship!

Are you both on the same page? Is there good give-and-take here? Do you both feel equally emotionally supported? Do you both contribute to the smooth domestic running of your home? Are you the only one picking up all the dirty socks? Who cleans the cat box?

The Justice card suggests fairness in relationship will be a theme in your life right now. Whether balance is achieved depends on the other cards in the spread. A lot of negative cards suggests that maybe you might be giving too much, but what does "too much" mean? Isn't that subjective?

It is! What matters is how you feel. This is a time when your purely subjective feelings have a great deal of weight, if only as a jumping off point to get to the heart of the matter. Issues of balance only feel bad when personal boundaries are crossed. If you feel like you are being taken for granted, then you have two choices: change your circumstance or change your perspective and, therefore, your attitude.

However, don't ignore this feeling. That is the seed of a wicked, resentful weed that will grow in all weather. Time to pay attention and realize that asking for what you need is important. You deserve to feel cherished, respected, and understood, as does your partner.

POSSIBLE OUTCOME

Fairness reigns! You succeed!

12: THE HANGED MAN

TRADITIONAL MEANING

A pause in the action. Needing to let go of all attempts to control. Sacrifice. Peaceful waiting. Submission.

LOVE READING

This is a card of fascinating contradictions. Its message is one of needing to behave in a way that is probably the opposite of what is instinctual for you.

The Hanged Man is here to tell you that this is a time where you cause more problems the more you struggle, cause more loss the more you "try." This is a time of letting go; not of the relationship, but of *any* attempts to control the outcome.

This is out of your hands. In a traditional Tarot deck, you will see that even though the man is suspended upside down, his face is serene. This is you. This needs to be you. In letting go, you win. In surrendering, you survive. If you are pushing someone hard to behave in a certain way, give you what you want to create a certain experience, or even to feel a certain way, then it will not succeed.

This is a delicate time, and whatever happens next will not be up to you. There are certain cards in the deck that strongly reinforce this idea. If The Fool, The High Priestess, Strength, or the restful Four of Swords show in the same reading, then you need to be cool as a cucumber: relax, be gentle with yourself, and let go of all demands.

If the Lovers card appears with this card, well, then you are really twisting in the wind, and the fate of this relationship is out of your hands.

Control is a tricky thing. It's like trying to sit on top of a beach ball while in a swimming pool: sure, you got that baby under water for now, but eventually it's going to pop up, and you are going down. Why not, instead, gently hold onto that ball as you skim the surface, letting it carry you across the water?

POSSIBLE OUTCOME

You don't get to know that right now! This is the Tarot's "Magic 8 Ball" equivalent of "Ask Again Later." Later, by the way, doesn't mean in an hour. Be still. Have faith. Let go. This is a card of beneficial outcome, but only if you stop struggling.

13: DEATH

TRADITIONAL MEANING

Radical change. Rebirth. New phase of life. Endings. Not a card of physical death.

LOVE READING

In spite of the less than cheerful nature of the Death card, I want to jump in here right now and tell you that NO, the Death card is not all bad! A lot depends on what else is in the spread!

Paired with The Lovers or The Two of Cups

For a single person, this means the end of loneliness!

Paired with the Wheel of Fortune

The end of bad luck!

Paired with The Magician, The Fool, The Five of Cups, The Eight of Cups, The Seven of Swords, The Ten of Swords, The Two of Swords, The Nine of Swords, Okay, Pretty Much All of The Swords

The end of the unhappy relationship you are trying really hard to make work in spite of the fact that it's really, deep down, a poor fit.

"Wait. What?"

I hear you now!

"NOOOO! I want this relationship to work out! Why can't this happen?! I want it! I love them! If I just make myself really, really tiny and don't take up any space, and just, you know, have no needs at all, for like, ever, then it will all work out!"

No. It's not going to happen. And my dear Reader and Querent, you don't want a different outcome than that, because you have something interesting and new just around the corner. That isn't a platitude. It is quite literally what the card means, traditionally. (Also, that relationship is BAD and it needs to GO and you deserve BETTER, my friend.)

And that is the best part about the Death card: in its finality, in its absolute change, comes a promise of new beginnings.

Just not with Chad. That guy's a dick.

POSSIBLE OUTCOME

Here you go! Off on a new adventure! Not with Chad!

14: TEMPERANCE

TRADITIONAL MEANING

Peace after struggle. Moderation. Simple life. Good choices.

LOVE READING

I often say this when I am doing a reading and Temperance shows up: "This is a card you don't appreciate as a teen, but crave as an adult." Why? Because it is a card of contentment, peace, plenty, and surviving a tough time and still coming out ahead. That sounds so BORING when you are young… but so, so delicious when you are an adult.

This is also true for naps.

There are many people who just don't feel ALIVE unless their love life is full of drama. They confuse peace with lack of chemistry, and so don't understand the pleasure of the easy relationship. This is not a card of boredom; this is a card of brunch, naps in hammocks on a Sunday, and good sex. Yay!

For the sane among us, who understand the value of this, Temperance is a very welcome card indeed. Temperance suggests that things go well, really well, and this is a person with whom you will even enjoy small, pleasant tasks, such as grocery shopping and running errands. You "get" each other, and feel emotionally comfy and safe.

It's a great card to see in a future aspect of a reading, as it means that no matter the struggles now, there is peace and happiness to come.

If health troubles are an aspect of your relationship, this card is a soothing omen of good health being on its way as well, and soon!

POSSIBLE OUTCOME

Best place for this card! No matter what, it's going to be okay and you will like the outcome. How cool is that?

15: THE DEVIL

TRADITIONAL MEANING

Oppression. Addiction. Obsession. Overindulgence. Difficult commitments.

LOVE READING

Okay! So, this one is hard to spin into an upside, for sure, but hey! Once again, there are many facets to the Major Arcana, and even The Devil card can have at least an interesting side.

Here's an aspect that might be exciting: The Devil is the card of kink! Are you a sexual adventurer? Open minded, as they say? Is your partner as well? GREAT! The Devil card suggests this is going to be an aspect of your romance that will be embraced with gusto.

Another possible positive is that The Devil symbolizes choices that are heavy, but ultimately positive, like taking on a mortgage or a marriage, in spite of being terrified. You are brave and strong and true!

But really, it pretty much stops there. The positive definitions above apply ONLY in a spread that is otherwise sunshine, wine, and roses. I mean it. Everything else in the spread needs to be unicorns and kittens.

If it is a mixed bag of dark and light, take the following cautions to heart: The Devil card shows up in readings where one partner is oppressive to another; is a narcissist; is verbally abusive, cruel or even physically abusive. I truly hope this goes without saying, but if this is the case, put down the cards and go. Don't read about this anymore. It's not going to get better. Take care of yourself and immediately get away. You can't fix this. You can't make it better.

This is also the card of addiction and overindulgence. If you are unhappy at home, it is natural to attempt to soothe yourself. Just do it in a wholesome way, and yes, wholesome most certainly includes the occasional martini. Occasional is not three a day.

POSSIBLE OUTCOME

Nope. Bad. No. Just... no.

16: THE TOWER

TRADITIONAL MEANING
Upheaval out of your control. Total collapse leading to rebirth. Outside forces affecting you.

LOVE READING
Well, the good news is that this is the last of the major bummer cards in the Major Arcana.

That is pretty much the only good news.

In a relationship spread, this card almost always means an ending is about to take place. The majority of the time, this is a breakup or a similar disappointment.

The Tower is a card of upheaval from the external world. You are not creating this, so if you can, take comfort in the fact that it is NOT your fault. This is a card of outside influences wreaking havoc on your relationship in some way: a layoff, a robbery, or an unexpected and painful breakup due to outside pressures. You are not the cause of the pain; you are just the lucky recipient of the poop sandwich.

Here's the other small comfort: The Tower card, no matter where it falls in a spread (past, present, or future position), it is always NOW. This reading is one of hours, days, a week or two at most. Whatever is about to happen is going to happen SOON, and the sooner it does, the sooner everyone can grab their brooms and start sweeping.

Is there ANY upside at all, here? Yes, but I hesitate to mention it, as it is rarely the case: sometimes The Tower is here to knock you on your butt in a good way. For example, you meet someone that is a life-changer and you both are gobsmacked and happy. YES, it happens, but rarely, so put the kettle on and know, deep in your hopeful heart, that it's most likely going to be a bumpy ride.

Finally, remember, Tarot speaks in bold and big symbols. Just because The Tower showed up, it doesn't mean that your entire life will collapse. Not at all. Sometimes it's a fight that leads to enlightenment and new understanding; sometimes the cat goes missing and you are both sad until you find one another again. It is not always catastrophe. Take heart!

POSSIBLE OUTCOME

Remember that part about breaking up? This position is when this is most likely. Time to book a massage and drink wine in the tub and Netflix binge for a little while. Onward and upward, Lover.

17: THE STAR

TRADITIONAL MEANING

Hope. Great happiness. Love given and love received. Bliss. Peace. Fulfillment.

LOVE READING

Well, now we're talking. The Star is one of the most positive and uplifting cards in the deck. There is no downside, and, in fact, like The Sun, it is considered such a good omen that it softens the effects of any other negative cards in the spread.

The Star is truly about hope, but it's also about gentleness, openheartedness, love freely given, and love gratefully received.

When paired with The Lovers
It can blind you to the little faults in your partner. That is not a bad thing, as I am not speaking of glaring faults, but possibly traits that might otherwise bother you. These are rose-colored glasses you don't want to take off, and you shouldn't! Enjoy!

When paired with The Tower
Look for what seems to be a huge loss in the realm of love as an incredible blessing in disguise.

Paired with The Sun
True kismet. This is easy, happy romance.

Paired with The Hierophant
Look for a romantic proposal soon.
The Star is a giver, and it is mostly a very feminine energy. There is also a sense of innocence, and a complete lack of hidden agenda. When this card shows up in your spread, you are lucky. What you see is what you get, and what you get is good!

POSSIBLE OUTCOME

No matter what it looks like now… keep hope alive. Wish granted!

18: THE MOON

TRADITIONAL MEANING

Dark feminine/mystery card. Occult magic. Fantasy. Illusion. Anxiety.

LOVE READING

Oh, The Moon. The Moon represents both the unknown and the willingness to entertain obsessive imaginings to soothe your worst fears and anxieties.

In a relationship, it can suggest that you are in a place of fantasy more than reality. You might ignore giant, waving red flags or live only in the future where your beloved finally commits and is emotionally present; is more romantic; suddenly wants sex again after a long, dry spell; or is simply not doing any of the confusing, heartbreaking things they have been doing so far.

And you! You are not off the hook here! What illusions are you nurturing regarding your own behavior? Have you blamed the other person entirely, not looking at the ways you create pain or distance in the relationship? Time to be gentle and open your eyes. Compassion is key, for both of you. Once you strip away the resentment and blame, you realize that everyone is having a different experience and isn't seeing what is happening between you in exactly the same way as you are. They might have perfectly good reasons for doing what they are doing that you simply can't see from your vantage point.

Unfurrow your brow and open your heart.

Dangerous place, the Realm of The Moon. When you live there, you live in hope, but be careful. It's not grounded in reality. I'm not saying there isn't a potential for a happy outcome, just know that whatever you imagine now might not necessarily be what is actually happening. Time to pay attention to what is really in front of you. You might be surprised.

POSSIBLE OUTCOME

A mystery! When this card appears in the outcome position, it means that the outcome is entirely uncertain, and will evolve over time. How frustrating! Hang in there, and be kind to each other in the meantime.

19: THE SUN

TRADTIONAL MEANING

Happiness. Joy. Pleasure. Favorable outcome. Transparency in all dealings. Childlike delight. The shiny light of truth.

ROMANCE READING

Glorious Sol! Here is an instance where the meaning of the card doesn't change much at all in a romance spread, and that's wonderful, because The Sun, along with The World, are the two most positive cards in the deck.

There is no downside to The Sun, except for the possibility that it is a flare of light, heat and pleasure that can burn itself out quickly, if not nurtured. This is the super-exciting new romance, the amazing first date, the moment you realize you both really are crazy about each other, but having these other cards appear in the spread can boost the power of this card, and make the outcome a bit more sustained:

Paired with The Hierophant
A strong mutual desire that deepens into commitment.

Paired with The Empress
For a man, you might have met "The One." For a couple hoping to conceive, this is particularly fortuitous.

Paired with The Two of Cups
A rich and exciting romance. Try not to go too fast.

Paired with The Magician
Your clever magnetism wins the heart of your intended.

Paired with The Ten of Swords
The pain you feel now will very soon feel like a distant memory.

Paired with The World

Yeah. It pretty much doesn't get better than this. Absolute triumph. Victory is yours! A winner is you!

Paired with The Devil
Your fears are unfounded or you quickly recognize the devil in your midst and remove him from your life. Let go, relax, and take good care of yourself.

Paired with The Seven of Swords
You will quickly see through any deception and come out on top.

Paired with The Six of Wands
Victory after struggle.

Paired with The Eight of Cups
You end something unsatisfying to which you once clung and valued highly and, in doing so, find new and great happiness.

Paired with Temperance
Entering a period of profound and sustained peace, plenty, and good health.

Paired with The Lovers
Great and true love. See a pattern here? Even in a "past" position in a spread, The Sun shines over all the cards in a reading, influencing them in a positive way.

POSSIBLE OUTCOME

Ideal. Whatever that might be for you.

20: JUDGMENT

TRADITIONAL MEANING

Big decision. Clarity with understanding. Leaving a dark time and entering a better phase of life. Choosing to let go of what no longer works. Absolution.

ROMANCE READING

The Judgment card is a very welcome card in any Tarot spread, especially as an outcome card. This is a card of promise that, after spending time in confusion, uncertainty, fear, or worry, you come to a fresh understanding that is a welcome comfort, relief, and new lease on life.

In a troubled relationship, it is a card that speaks of deepening connection, forgiveness, good communication, and "Okay, let's do this thing!"-thinking.

This is a card about picking a side and making a choice. Choosing is important. Ambivalent feelings about a relationship are very damaging if they go on too long. If you or your partner have one foot in, and one foot out, it feels like you are playing it safe and protecting yourself or another from hurt, or controlling the flow of the relationship, but it actually is very eroding. It can create the very thing that keeps you fearful in the first place.

Ambivalence keeps things from deepening, emotionally, and it also stifles the small, comforting, everyday "we are in this together"-feelings and pleasantly conspiratorial experiences that make a relationship feel real, safe, and sturdy enough to stand on. It creates insecurity and neediness even in the most stalwart heart. It kills passion.

When you aren't really choosing, nothing grows between you. Untapped potential stops ripening on the vine and starts to whither, instead.

Judgment is coming down off the fence after much reflection and saying, "Well, I don't know what's going to happen, but I am here, and I want you with me." As scary as that can feel, it creates a safe space, emotionally, to find out a romance's true potential. This is a great place to be, and this card suggests that you choose and, in turn, are chosen. You forgive and are forgiven. Slate cleaned and moving forward! What you do with that opportunity is up to you!

POSSIBLE OUTCOME

Clarity after confusion! The clouds part! You choose to go forward or *you choose to leave*, but, in the act of choosing, you find happiness and peace.

21: THE WORLD

TRADITIONAL MEANING

Ending of one phase to begin a new, brilliant life. Absolute fulfillment. Happiness.

LOVE READING

Oh, The World! How I love The World! It is, most simply, the best card in the deck.

What's fun about The World is that, while there are a number of cards that are very upbeat and happy and about good things coming (The Sun, The Star, The Nine of Cups, The Aces of every suit), The World brings with its promise of great satisfaction an added layer of deep fulfillment.

So, it's happiness that lasts and change that is positive and consistent in its benefits. It is a long stretch of good luck. In a world that is endlessly changing at the drop of a hat, with each day stuffed to the gills with wave after wave of expectations, pressures, overwhelming and often useless "information" from media that batters our brains around like tennis balls, The World says, "Hey, this thing? This experience? You get to keep it for a while. Enjoy."

The World is also about achievement. So you pass through a time that was challenging, such as graduate school, a hard internship, a tricky job situation, or a complicated dating situation, and a true and measurable shift occurs, and the results are beautiful. The hard work pays off. Things gently and easily fall into place.

Good stuff!

POSSIBLE OUTCOME

Again, best card in the deck. The World as your outcome card is the most welcome card you could see, regardless of the topic of the reading. It's the embodiment of "YES!" after a long period of struggle.

THE WANDS

Image copyright J. Daniels with elements used with permission.

In traditional definitions of Tarot, the Wands are about creativity, work, and communication.

In relationships this continues, with a heavy emphasis on communication, issues of power, balance, and sex!

ACE OF WANDS

TRADITIONAL MEANING

A new creative process. Starting a new business. A grand beginning.

ROMANCE READING

This is a theme I will return to at the beginning of each of the four suits, but it should always be kept in mind that the Ace of any suit is the purest, most distilled form of the fundamental attributes of the suit itself. It also symbolizes the new, so think new influences, new people, and new ways of doing things. In this way, change is good, even for change-fighters like, oh, most of us. Even when we get to the dark and contemplative Swords, there is still reason for hope, as you will learn as you read on!

Aces are always welcome. They soften the blows of the dark cards and add to the positive cards with new, fresh, and concentrated energy.

To start, the Ace of Wands is clearly a phallic symbol. For those of us who appreciate the phallus, this is nice. You have the hots for each other. Sexual mojo.

In a love reading, the Ace of Wands suggests a new beginning, whether in the form of a new romance, or a new phase in an existing one. It also suggests strong sexual chemistry, regardless of whether your relationship is one of opposite or same gender. Even more, er, lastingly, it suggests excellent, easy, non-stressful communication, which is a sorely underrated bit of wonderfulness.

If you have something important to say to someone special, the Ace of Wands is here to tell you that you have the skills to communicate effectively, charmingly, and possibly to the point of removal of clothing, you sweet-talking devil!

POSSIBLE OUTCOME

Sexy times for you, with lots of warm connection to follow! This one's a cuddler!

TWO OF WANDS

TRADITIONAL MEANING

Imposition of power. All the responsibility, but none of the authority. Bluffing in order to seem important.

ROMANTIC READING

Are you trying to impose your will on another? Is someone trying to control the relationship in a stubborn or selfish manner? The dull, often pedantic and mildly crazy-making oppressiveness of the Two of Wands suggests that some rather tiresome, insecure behavior is at hand. Sure, you or they might get their way, but it's at great expense, such as the respect another might have for you.

This is the mean little brother of the worst aspects of The Chariot, so if they are in the same spread, watch out for thoughtless and selfish behavior. These are petty control issues and unreasonable expectations, such as needing to know where your partner is at all times, expecting texts to be answered instantly, or needing three calls a day. Super fun, and WAY conducive to romance, no?

POSSIBLE OUTCOME

Meh, on it's own. The tiresome behavior listed above continues. Carefully look at the other cards in the spread to see how this might play out. Lots of happy cards suggest this is just a blip, but mixed or negative spreads suggest you might be falling for a rigid and controlling person…unless that person is you! *YOU ARE NOT THAT PERSON*. You are so much cooler than that. You are secure, calm, trusting with time and utterly trustworthy yourself, and wow, that's really attractive, isn't it?

THREE OF WANDS

TRADITIONAL MEANING

Excellent leadership. New, positive levels of responsibility coming to you. New opportunities to show off your skills.

ROMANTIC READING

Ah. This is the card the Two of Wands pretends to be, but fails. This is someone who is competent, calm and kind, and it's the nice little brother of the Strength card. This means enjoying the comfort that comes with a person who is a grown up or a situation that is comforting and competent.

This is the man that makes the reservations, shows up on time, and smells like soap and good manners (they smell like victory), but who might also have hidden, sexy tattoos underneath his crisp, button-down shirt. This man knows what he is about. He's a good kisser. He takes good care of his pets. He can cook at least one really good meal. He wants to cook it for you.

As a situation, it means dating someone who makes you feel like an adult having a good time, rather than a kid playing at dating. Relax, and enjoy.

POSSIBLE OUTCOME

Yes. Keep seeing this person. This card with the Three of Pentacles or any good Cups card is sturdy romantic stuff, indeed.

FOUR OF WANDS

TRADITIONAL MEANING

Engagement, happy home life, new home, surprise happiness.

ROMANTIC READING

Oh, this is a little sweetie of a card. In a traditional deck, it shows two couples dancing under a chuppah, which is the small, four-posted tent-like structure used in a Jewish wedding. This is a card of celebration, a happy surprise that is not an *unexpected* outcome, but one that is even *BETTER* than your hopeful expectations.

It doesn't mean marriage, necessarily, but it certainly does mean a happy union, and it's a wonderful omen to show up in any spread. Paired with the Lovers or Two of Cups or Hierophant, though…yes, a commitment might be on the table, whether it's the very first levels of this, such as romantic exclusivity, or even the Whole Beautiful Terrifying Catastrophe we won't even name yet (because we aren't getting ahead of ourselves, are we?). It certainly bodes well for any romance.

POSSIBLE OUTCOME

Happy Surprise! Fun! Celebration! Going Steady! Being claimed!

FIVE OF WANDS

TRADITIONAL MEANING

Competition. Playful fighting but hey, you might take an eye out! Struggle.

LOVE READING

Do you like to be right?

By this I mean, do you like to be right more than you like to be happy?

..and by *THIS* I mean, are you aware that beating someone into submission with a verbal *Hammer of Self Righteousness* is not actually conducive to intimacy or closeness?

Or, are you under the hammer yourself? No good. Someone is overwhelming someone else with a need to win at all costs. Even if they, or you, might think it's playful banter, it's actually exhausting to the other person. Both of your needs matter equally. If not, it's really just mental masturbation for the person doing the hammering.

Don't let your desire to be heard turn into a need to shut up your partner.

POSSIBLE OUTCOME

Hm. Changeable. You are stuck right in the middle of the battle of wills. I wish I could tell you who will win, but I can't. And in love, really, shouldn't both of you win? This might just be a single argument, so don't fret. Just pay attention, with careful, measured observation.

SIX OF WANDS

TRADITIONAL READING

Victory. Triumph. Winning.

ROMANCE READING

So. This is a card of happiness and a sense of achievement. In traditional Tarot a knight is riding through town in the center of a parade, with banners and laurel wreaths all around him. Good stuff, but it is possibly of the shallow sort.

This is the first flush of triumph in a new relationship, a sense of "getting the girl." Negatively, you might feel like you are dating someone you think is "out of your league."

No such thing. No one is out of anyone's dang league! People either fit in a good match of character, interests, sexual attraction, morals, emotional needs, and expressions thereof, or they don't, but people are just people. Everyone is a hairless biped. That biped you are putting on a pedestal does goofy stuff alone when no one is watching, just like you do.

POSSIBLE OUTCOME

Be careful of idealizing either the person you want, or the relationship itself. Yes, this is a card of accomplishment, but not a card of emotional connection, so this is just a first step. Enjoy it, by all means, enjoy -- just know that it's only a great first signpost.

In Even Better News:

In a well-established relationship, it might simply mean a lovely victory that has you both celebrating together. Someone gets a great new job! Someone passes the bar examination! Someone takes a risk and it pays off for both of you! Cork popping to commence!

SEVEN OF WANDS

TRADITIONAL MEANING

Fighting alone, against a group, and winning.

ROMANCE READING

Seriously, more fighting? Ugh.

Tiresome, I know, but relationships, especially more challenging ones, often require more corrections of balance or difficult confrontations. Knowing if that's a worthy challenge or a futile one takes a bit of time.

I know. Sucks.

Depending on the placement of this card, it might be the card of a person being more trouble, in the end, than enhancement in your life. Of course you deserve success in love and life and to be happy. It would be so great to tell you this is all going to work out, but sometimes things just go wonky for nebulous, frustrating manifestations – or simply a poor fit. This is especially true in a spread with many Swords.

On the plus side, with any of the positive Cup cards, this can mean you team up, fight the good fight against outside foes and difficult life obstacles, and bond together in a positive way. It can happen! Carefully look to other cards in the spread to see if this might be the interpretation you can grab with your hot little hands.

POSSIBLE OUTCOME

Hm. Don't lose heart, but really DO step back and drop your stick. Everyone needs to drop his or her stick (schtick?) and breathe a bit. Calm WAY down. Remember, this is not your adversary. This is another person, someone you LIKE, struggling to get needs met, just as you are.

EIGHT OF WANDS

TRADITIONAL MEANING

Rapid, sometimes overwhelming movement. Big change, happening very quickly.

ROMANCE READING

Oh man, this is going really fast!

If this is a NEW relationship:

Buckle up, Buttercup, because you are about to be swept up in a whirlwind. Sometimes, this is freaking GREAT, and all you need do is hold on and laugh, because you have found yourself a perfect match and it all falls into place because It Simply Can't Help Itself.

This is rapid movement, sometimes of the overwhelming sort. Super fun, right? Right!

Just...be careful, because this is *new*.

Be careful, especially, oh dear *especially*, if The Emperor, the Magician or ANY of the Knights are in a reading with this card. Knights are all about rapidity and change, which is fun, but in this case, it might be a situation of rapid seduction with even more rapid departure. Keep your head, Lover. Slow *DOWN*. Pay *ATTENTION*.

If this is a longer term relationship:

YAY! Unstuck! Your relationship was a four-wheeler stuck in the mud, and the Eight of Wands is the friendly tow truck that just happens to drive by. Change, movement, busy-ness and business move rapidly, invigorating the both of you. New life, new experiences, and with those new experiences, fresh eyes. Good stuff.

POSSIBLE OUTCOME

Everything I said above? It goes double, here.

NINE OF WANDS

TRADITIONAL MEANING

Pause before the final battle. Readying yourself. Exhaustion.

ROMANCE READING

Oh dear. It appears that either a relationship, or a situation within the relationship, might be causing so much stress that it is hanging on by a single thread.

This is more work than fun. You are not quite ready to throw in the towel yet, but it feels as if one more crummy thing happens, just one more, *it* will be *it* and *you* will be *gone*. You really mean it this time, dammit!

This is the card of the person who stays loyal when others would have gone, stays in when others would have long ago moved on. Sometimes it works out. Sometimes hanging in is a good thing, and you get past this very tough time.

You have the strength for one more go. One. You mean it. Really. But dang, you are pooped.

POSSIBLE OUTCOME

You are right on the brink. I'm sorry. It's a painful and exhausting way to feel. Is your partner or romantic interest supportive of your emotional needs? Are they trying? I don't mean words. I mean action? Then, by all means, stay.

If they aren't, and you are there in spite of little encouragement or support, please remember to take very good care of *you*, given it appears you are the only one doing so. Also, don't do that too much longer, Star Pirate. Here There Be Dragons.

TEN OF WANDS

TRADITIONAL MEANING

Taking on far too much. Martyrdom. Out of fuel. Being ground down.

ROMANCE READING

In the card that comes before this I wrote that you had one more "go" to give.

Well, this is the place that is WELL beyond that.

This is taking on *way too much*, doing all the heavy lifting in a relationship, and being the person whom people take for granted. It's feeling very ground down, possibly resentful, and totally exhausted.

Sexy, huh?

Sometimes, only one person is holding the two of you together because one of you is in trouble. Whether it is suppressing your basic emotional needs for the sake of peace, or doing all the dang housework, it's about doing too much, and gross imbalance.

Sometimes people like to be the person who does too much, and this can relate to issues of control. Sometimes it's an unconscious way to keep distance, because how can you go deeper when everything is a mess?

POSSIBLE OUTCOME

There are many complicated psychological reasons why this unbalanced dynamic might feel like "home" to you, but just because it is your past, it does not mean it needs to be your future.

Consider the possibility that "things going well" might be secretly terrifying for you. The higher expectations, the scary vulnerability, the unconscious fear of abandonment and loss that real intimacy can sometimes inspire can be terrifying, but that's where the good stuff is too. The Best Stuff.

Please consider yourself worthy of the good stuff!

THE WAND COURT CARDS

The Court Cards of the Suit of Wands are considered to be the most appealing of the four suits, because they tend to be the most balanced and emotionally intelligent. There is a bit more *Strum und Drang* in the suits to follow (not TOO much, mind you), but these folks tend to be pretty even keeled.

Traditional Meanings and Romantic meanings blend when it comes to the Court. I will keep the focus on the romantic when we are dealing with the royalty.

PAGE OF WANDS

ROMANTIC READING

Traditionally a young person, female or male. A very young romance. Pages, as a situation, speak of important communication that shifts a situation in a different direction, but in the case of the Wands, this is less emotional and more practical. News changes circumstances in a positive way. The warm letter. The new contract. The good news.

As a person this could be you, if you are a young woman especially, or if more mature, it could be a young person associated with your romantic interest, such as their child. This is a nice person who is often accomplished, smart, and driven. Traditionally, they represent someone who might have blond or light brown colored hair, and medium toned skin. Attractive, and in a pretty much universally appealing way.

POSSIBLE OUTCOME

The Page brings news that brings good cheer. Kind young person in your life.

KNIGHT OF WANDS

ROMANTIC READING

Here would be your Golden God. He's hunky and charming and good. He might be a bit clueless because he might have been so blessed genetically (and by life) that he just assumes everyone is as happy as he is, though not every Knight of Wands is traditionally handsome. As a romantic interest, well, he's pretty dreamy to most people, even more for what's inside.

Not usually the intellectual, but not dumb. Not even close. He makes others feel at ease, and cares about the well-being of others. He is earnest and kind, optimistic and extroverted.

As a situation, a Knight is always about the rapid approach of excitement and change. Being swept up. Sometimes this can bring with it seduction and abandonment, but the Knight of Wands is usually a pretty good man. He's sincere.

POSSIBLE OUTCOME

Excitement and change. New energy, or a new man. Rapid advancement in a relationship.

QUEEN OF WANDS

ROMANTIC READING

She is what used to be known as a "classy broad." Elegant, stylish and warm, she is often successful in business, accomplished, and very smart. She is an excellent partner and friend, confident, pretty fearless, and often entrepreneurial. Again, tends to be light brown to blond hair, and medium skin, but that is just a traditional idea, and hardly applicable to everyone.

As a situation, it suggests that there is more than enough emotional intelligence here to handle most communication issues. She is a very kind and benevolent presence. She's a catch.

POSSIBLE OUTCOME

Court cards as outcome cards tend to be nebulous, and often simply mean "add these attributes to the mix." If you are mad for her (and you know she represents a specific person), having her in the outcome position tends to suggest that longing might be returned. Lucky you!

If you are looking for love, but currently single, she might be the person that is on the way.

KING OF WANDS

ROMANTIC READING

So, take everything that is appealing about the Knight of Wands and bring it here, but add to the witch's cauldron the following: Emotional intelligence tempered even further with maturity and experience, a career or hobbies and interests enjoyed and pursued with gusto. Even better, add warmth, confidence, emotional availability, and a healthy sex drive, well into later years.

Bubble, bubble, no toil, no trouble.

As a situation, he simply means everyone involved is a grownup, and communication is good. Add him to Strength, and wow! Jackpot!

POSSIBLE OUTCOME

If you are looking for love, hold on to your hat. If you are interested in him and know who he is, the King of Wands in this position suggests a real romance might be on the table. He's going to be fun.

THE SUIT OF CUPS

Image copyright J. Daniels with elements used with permission.

Now we are at home. We come now to the suit that deals directly and easily with romance, emotions, watery deep feelings, creativity and right brain creative activity. Poets and artists and designers, pay attention, as well as those of you who wish they were poets and artists and designers. The second part of that sentence is worth remembering when we get to the court cards!

Here you will find that traditional definitions and the romantic definitions that are the focus of this book have a great deal of similarity, but let's EXPAND on this a bit, and find richer meaning where we can!

THE ACE OF CUPS

TRADITIONAL MEANING

New love, the beginning of a creative adventure, hot new emotions. ROMANCE.

ROMANTIC READING

Ah. How nice. Lucky you. Just what you want, and it doesn't matter where it lands. Again, aces are always the most concentrated form of the essence of their suit, so here is a big boost to the romance factor.

Aces are new beginnings, so this card showing up in a reading means either that a new romance is on it's way, has just arrived, or, in an established relationship, a new and romantic phase or experience is about to begin. A second honeymoon!
This card is a super booster. It softens sad blows and gives the good cards more oomph. If the Lovers card, the Two of Cups, or the Nine of Cups show up with this, there is a "wish come true" factor to this combination, but be careful what you wish for. Want that guy or girl just so bad? Are you sure? It's always best to pay more attention to whether or not you like them, rather than if they like you!

Should Knights, Kings, Queens or the Emperor or Empress show up in a spread with this card, look carefully at the card, its attributes, its personality, because this is a big indicator of the specifics of the Person of Romantic Interest who might appear.

Should the Three of Wands, Three of Pentacles, Four of Wands, the Ten of Pentacles, or the Hierophant show up with this card, there is a great chance of "Happily Ever After," and possibly some life changing commitment that causes you both to thrive.

POSSIBLE OUTCOME

Oh wow…how exciting! The game is afoot! This is a real romance! A caveat: This is JUST the "stars-in-your-eyes, everything-they-do-is-perfect" beginning, lover, so keep your head on straight while you see if this has legs!

TWO OF CUPS

TRADTIONAL MEANING

Falling in love. Transformative love. Profound exchange of affection, fidelity and passion. A superb partnership in business or play. Great working environment. INFATUATION.

ROMANTIC READING

Yay! This is the little sister to the Lovers card, with the absence of momentous choice between two loves or life upheavals that often come with the Lovers.

What you have left are the pure and sweet aspects of new romance. Where the Two of Swords, as we will come to see, is all about withholding love and rejection of same, the Two of Cups is all generosity, all passion, all pet names and long stares and enough sex to have you walking funny.

And yes, that is all marvelous and stupendous but let's take a moment to be deeply grateful that this is a temporary insanity. Imagine if this initial infatuation never settled down into something a bit more real. NOTHING WOULD GET DONE, anywhere. People would starve, no work would be accomplished, everyone would be nuts. Naked and nuts.

So thank goodness this settles down a bit. NOW, whether it does settle down into hot, low embers or just winks itself out in a flash like a burning piece of paper on the wind depends on the cards around it, and of course, the behavior of people in question. This is a card of emotional greed, so be careful. Don't gobble each other up in one experience. Take your time.

Cards that indicate a possible flash in the pan: Five of Wands (possible seduction for seduction's sake), The Fool, The Magician, The Tower, The Devil, Seven or Swords (duplicity), Nine of Swords (infidelity) and the Seven of Cups (self delusion and fantasy).

Cards that indicate a possibility of long term romance and slow burning fires: The Lovers, The Eight of Pentacles (commitment and slow growth), the Three of Pentacles (building something together, living together), Four of Wands (proposals), Hierophant (same!), The Sun (because SUN) and The Star.

POSSIBLE OUTCOME

The Two of Cups is in a perfect spot when reading for the outcome of a romance. It does not guarantee an "and they lived Happily Ever After" sort of outcome, because we Star Pirates are very grounded in even our romantic fantasy, yes? But this bodes VERY well indeed for you. New romance is coming, big time.

THREE OF CUPS

TRADITIONAL READING

Celebration, Wedding, Friendship, Over-indulgence, New Friends.

ROMANTIC READING

The meaning of this card is unchanged in this aspect. This is a card of weddings, celebration, friendship, a feeling of being part of a group, being accepted and wanted by a group, and possible overindulgence in spending and food and drink.

SO, what does this mean for you in a romance spread?

Well, it could actually be very practical! You will be going to a wedding! Friends you really care for will be there. One of them might have a single and charming friend. Flirting could happen!

Mostly though, it speaks of being emotionally well supported by people who love and care for you. In a romance spread it could also mean that your friends are the conduit through which you meet a Romantic Interest, so keep your eyes peeled in a, you know, super casual, totally self confident, no big deal sort of way.

Because love ain't everything, my fellow travelers, and your friends will be there long after a passing flirtation passes by.

POSSIBLE OUTCOME

Celebration is definitely on the menu. In fact, in the outcome position, this celebration might very well be your own. Take good care of your friends, and remember not to neglect them when you fall in love!

FOUR OF CUPS

TRADITIONAL MEANING

Self-absorption and dissatisfaction with how things are going. A failure to notice what is good and in front of you.

ROMANCE READING

Well. Hm. Someone is behaving rather badly.

Is it you, or is it the object of your romantic intentions? Where this card falls in your reading will more easily tell you which of you it is, but regardless: someone needs a shake up!

Why? Well, the Four of Cups is a card that speaks of lack of perspective, lack of empathy, and nearly crippling self-absorption. Even worse, the core meaning of this card is an inability to see and appreciate what is right in front of you.

In a traditional Four of Cups card, maybe like the one you have in front of you right now, you will see a rather petulant looking youth sitting under a tree, looking entirely morose. There are three full goblets in front of him, and even more telling, a fourth one being held in front of him by a disembodied, angelic hand, and he doesn't even notice! What a weenie!
Do you have someone wonderful in your life who has many, many great qualities but you are considering rejecting him/her over a very small attribute? Is your own star-shiny wonderfulness being ignored by that self absorbed person you are sure, just absolutely SURE, you can get to love you if only you're just a bit more...perfect?

If you are the rejecter (the weenie), carefully examine your own behavior. Maybe, sure, there is something profoundly and fundamentally wrong with this romance, and it's time to go. But just maybe not.

You just might be rejecting someone great because you have an idealized version of what you think your true love will be, and if anyone falls short of this ideal, you are outta there. It's a great way to avoid actual intimacy, isn't it? Effective.

On the other side of this coin, you might just be dating a Jerkface. It's true that sometimes, when life throws us for a loop, we don't manifest our very best selves. People who are scared or worried or sad can be temporary Jerkfaces until they get it together. Sometimes though, your Romantic Hopeful gets stuck there and manifests as Jerkface 24/7. Take careful note! It's not your job to fix this. Not your circus; not your monkeys.

POSSIBLE OUTCOME Prepare for withdrawal or disappointment. I am sorry. Time to run a bath, pronto.

FIVE OF CUPS

TRADITIONAL MEANING

Disappointment. Loss, with something left over.

ROMANCE READING

Well, poop.

I DO actually have an upside bunny to pull from my magic hat for this card, but I am going to have to reach around a bit before I find it.

A traditional depiction of this card is a man with his face down at a table, three goblets turned over, two full goblets on a shelf behind him.

Is he drunk and behaving badly? Is he sad? Is he sad because he can't drink the last two goblets and wants them because he is greedy and self-indulgent? These are all aspects of this card that can manifest. Not in actual drunkenness, but in bad choices, disappointment in your own behavior or the behavior of others. Also, tantalizingly, the idea could be that not all is lost.

The good news is this is not a card of devastation, or even a particularly powerful card. It is weak, fundamentally, and this means that it is easily mitigated by the cards around it. It also means that the sorrow depicted can be of a shallow sort. A bad fight. Some cruel words exchanged. Not getting something you wanted, but this lack of something is not devastating to you.

Also, remember this: there are still two full cups left. This means that you have not lost it all. You have just taken three steps back. Time to take two steps forward …and then keep going, because there is a chance this is salvageable….and you are this close to dancing!

POSSIBLE OUTCOME

This is an unfortunate placement for this card, as it does mean the good times are not coming…yet. But don't lose heart. Forewarned is forearmed, and knowing this blow up is on its way might be just the thing needed to dodge it in the first place!

SIX OF CUPS

TRADITIONAL MEANING

Nostalgia. Old friends. Returning home. A sense of safety or comfort.

ROMANTIC READING

Ah. A nice little break in a small streak of rather glum cards. The Six of Cups is not a card of portent by its lonesome. It's not a very strong card at all. But what it is… is good. It's friendly. It's familiar. It's kind and comfortable and well known. It's toast and milky tea. It's a grilled cheese sandwich and tomato soup.

The Six of Cups is here to gently remind you, Star Pirate, that while it might be fun to adventure upon the High Seas of Love, sometimes you need to take a break. Watch an old favorite movie. Maybe go for a long walk with your dog who is, by now, giving you the hairy fish eye because some other "snookums" has gobbled up all your mental rental space for a good long while.

(Dogs remember when you had baby talk only for them, thank you very much. They haven't pooped in your shoes yet, because they love you so, so much. But they have had, shall we say, dark fantasies.)

This is the card of self care, hanging out with friends and family and people who love you already and don't want to get into your pants.

Now, of course, because this is Love Tarot, there is an angle to this card that might be romantic. When this card shows up in a reading, it MIGHT possibly mean that you meet a quiet, cute guy or girl through an old friend. Could also mean an old friend starts looking …different these days. How did you not notice the line of his jaw before? Did she always have those eyes? Whoa.

It's possible. Look for other romantic cards in the spread. If they show up too (especially The Star), it can mean that the person you dig is a comfy and familiar soul indeed. Soul mate? Whoo!

POSSIBLE OUTCOME

In this position, all things listed above still have relevance, but there is an added emphasis on home and self care. Don't worry, adventurer, you can ride the stormy seas again soon enough. Grilled cheese and trusting dog's bellies: Don't underestimate their power.

SEVEN OF CUPS

TRADITIONAL MEANING

Illusion. Delusion. Fantasy. Wishful thinking. Sensual indulgence.

ROMANTIC READING

Some of us want love so much we are in love with love itself. That is the essence of the Seven of Cups.

In non-romantic spreads this card is the card of either too much earthly self-indulgence, or being all talk, and no action. It could even mean we are self-delusional with regard to our own efficacy.

In love readings, it is all of these aspects as well, but it manifests as a desire to have love so badly we might paint a thin, glittery coating of it over someone we don't know very well. We might throw it at someone onto whom we project many fine qualities that might be there, or might simply be a collage of our hopes and desires.

Ever fallen hard for someone almost instantly, and they the same with you? Maybe it IS love. It is most certainly absolutely possible, and far be it from me to say that you haven't been hit with the true thunderbolt. I believe in The Thunderbolt. I do!

But sometimes it feels like love, and it's intoxicating, and you both go nuts, gobble it all up, and then poof! It's gone. You both are dropped on your butts, scratching your heads, and wondering just what the heck happened there. Where did all the feelings go?

You are both lovely people. You just aren't the people you thought you were "loving." You are the people who fall in love at the masquerade ball, and then find that in the light of day, in your street clothes, you have no idea who this real person is.

Heartbreaking, I know.

So, when you see this card in the future position, don't close down, just remember that this is the very beginning. Remember that yes, they are so very shiny, and that's marvelous! Enjoy it, and then look deeper, and get to know the real person there. That real person might be wonderful too.

POSSIBLE OUTCOME

Seriously. Watch that projection stuff. Infatuation is a POWERFUL DRUG, but it does wear off, and the hangover is a bear. Both feet on the ground, please!

EIGHT OF CUPS

TRADITIONAL MEANING

Losing faith. Leaving to start anew. Letting go of things that were at one time very important.

ROMANTIC READING

One of the strangest aspects to the human adventure is the idea that one can have the experience of loving so strongly, feeling a devotion so deeply, and KNOWING in your heart of hearts that this is how you will feel forever and nothing will change and this is YOU, baby! This is Your Truth with a capital T!

Right up until the moment where it's not.

Some things are simply not going to last forever, and it is always such a confusing and sometimes shocking realization.

The Eight of Cups is about change, often of the resigned and hard to come by sort, in that it is the perfect expression of the moment when you realize that the person, situation, or goal to which you were once endlessly fascinated and loyally devoted has become untenable, and you are going to need to let go.

In a traditional Tarot card a man walks away from eight cups, late at night, while a sad moon looks on, but this is not necessarily a bad thing.

Sometimes we stay way, way too long at the party. Sometimes we are loyal to a relationship that doesn't deserve our loyalty. This is the card that speaks of the moment when you decide your heart matters too, and it's time to go.

There is promise in this card of new devotions. This is not a card of desolation. This is a card about the moment you decide to protect your heart and get it to a safe place so that you can love again.

POSSIBLE OUTCOME

Yes. You are letting go, or soon will be doing so. Know in your heart that you are making a good choice that is coming from good self-care, and that you will be able to love again.

NINE OF CUPS

TRADITIONAL MEANING

The Wish Card. Wish come true. Careful what you wish for!

ROMANTIC READING

When you get a tarot reading, this is the card you hope pops up. It is the "Happily Ever After" card, and very much Wish Granted. But, what happens to the princess once she rides off in the carriage?

Before you go skipping along to the land of "Pop Tarts and Yoohoo for Breakfast", let's be very, very careful about what you are wishing for, because you might actually get it.

So, you want that man, or that woman, and you get them, and oh yeah, surprise, they are maybe not so nice, or lousy in bed, or actually, once you get past their great good looks, kind of stupid.

You want that affair with that married boss of yours? Wish come true! Now, you're fired. Good times.

I'm not saying that the Nine of Cups is the Monkey's Paw of Tarot cards, with an ironic and painful twist of an outcome just around the corner. I'm just saying that wanting something isn't the same as knowing what is best for you, so be careful. The Nine of Cups can be woozy, self indulgent and short lived in its manifestation, so look for grounding cards like Temperance, the Three of Pentacles, Three of Wands, Strength, The Sun, or The World. All of these cards are about moderation, maturity and good choices.

Still, if the basis of your desires is wholesome, as it were, this is a very welcome card indeed. So go ahead and be delighted. Delight is fun.

POSSIBLE OUTCOME

This is considered the very best placement for this card, bar none. When the Nine of Cups lands in the outcome position, you will be celebrating. Wish come true.

TEN OF CUPS

TRADITIONAL MEANING

Happily ever after. Satisfying home life. Prosperity and plenty. Security and beauty.

ROMANTIC READING

Now this is a straight up glorious card to have in any reading, period. Doesn't matter where it lands in a spread, either. In the past, it means you have a great foundation for your coming happiness, in the present you are THERE and it's all about to happen, and in the future, oh boy, so welcome. *Laissez les bon temps rouler!*

What is truly wonderful about the promise of the Ten of Cups is that it signifies not only pleasure, prosperity and happiness, it is a promise of *lasting* pleasure, prosperity and happiness.

Yes, life is about change, for sure, and rolling with the punches of this change is a beautiful skill we all need to have to thrive, but this is a kind and gentle nudge from the universe that says this is something that is not only going to pan out in an ideal way, but is something you get to keep for a while.

Lucky, lucky you!

If the Ten of Cups shows up with any of these cards, expect your happiness to be even more grounded and rich in expression: Sun, Ten of Pentacles, Three of Pentacles, The Star, Three of Wands, Strength, Temperance, Two of Cups, and yes, even the tricky and fun Nine of Cups. (That is a rare combination.)

Pair this card with ANY of the Aces and you are even luckier. Any of the Court Cards, and you know who is responsible.

Even dark cards are strongly lightened. The Nine of Swords? Turns out your worries are just worries, rather than reality. The Three of Swords? The sad news you receive turns out to be one of the best things that can happen to you, in the end. The Tower? The overdue clearing away of garbage to make way for new prosperity.

There is no downside to this card whatsoever.

POSSIBLE OUTCOME

No, really, you are a lucky, lucky duck. Enjoy that.

COURT CARDS OF THE SUIT OF CUPS

While Court Cards are often symbols of actual people, they too are symbols of experience, and most especially so with the Cups.

PAGE OF CUPS

TRADITIONAL MEANING

Young, sensitive person. Love letters, romantic news. A proposal.

ROMANTIC READING

While the Page of Cups can often be easily seen as a young and idealistic person in your life, I have found that far more often this particular Page is more about an experience you are having or are about to have.

The Page of Cups is a charming symbol of new love rushing in. Sweet, tender, open, giving and innocent, this romance is sincere, mutual and loving. How glorious this is in a modern world that seems to be made of hookups and chill.

This is mushy text messages and three-hour phone calls and infatuation and kindness. You walk around with little clouds on your feet (to quote my sweetie at the beginning of our romance), bouncing along with each step. Good stuff, and genuine, rather than mere seduction.

POSSIBLE OUTCOME

Oh how nice. New romance. GREAT placement for this card, as it means you might be on the precipice of an Awfully Big Adventure. Enjoy!

KNIGHT OF CUPS

TRADITIONAL MEANING

Swift action and change. Romantic young man, dashing and poetic. Seduction.

ROMANTIC MEANING

Okay, Star Pirate, time to put your Reality Goggles on, because it's very, very easy to get swept up right now.

Of all the Knights this one is the most dangerous, because he is the most charming. The Knight of cups is the Seducer, the Handsome Cad, the Wounded Poet, the Talented Yet Perpetually Unemployed Musician, and every other rogue-ish stereotype you can imagine.

And YES, he could ALSO be a tender, loving, genuine, warm dollface you should snatch up like the smartypants you are and never let go. Absolutely. He is rare and to be cherished. At his best the Knight of Cups is a romantic and tender lover, a great communicator, a true romantic, and a real mensch. He tends to be dark haired and light skinned, but this is only a traditional interpretation and certainly should be low on "traits that are true" list.

POSSIBLE OUTCOME

Keep those shiny eyes wide open, and pay attention. Sometimes this Knight swoops in with speed, seduces with skill, and then is gone in a puff of confusion and surprised disappointment. This applies to all knights but one: the Pentacles. Keep your wits about you!

QUEEN OF CUPS

TRADITIONAL READING

Gracious, charming, creative woman. Romantic experiences.

ROMANCE MEANING

Ah. She's a charmer. At her best, the Queen of Cups is a sort of magic pixie dream girl, full of wit and delight and creative expression and sensuality and playfulness and whoo, she's *fine*.

At her worst, she's a bit moody and petulant and self absorbed and overly sensitive, and whoo, she's *a little crazy*.

It's that kind of crazy that makes men nuts (in a good way) and other women confused, but she is certainly attractive in a big way.

This queen is the artist and seducer of the Tarot. Delightful, quick, witty and sweet, she is intoxicating and sexy and you are dazzled by her many talents.

As a situation, think of her as romance personified. She is the great date that seals the deal, the "taking it to the next step" moment, the sparkling romance that is full of light and sensuality and sex.

Not that she's all pink and glitter, mind you. She can be gothy or nerdy or the smoldering sexpot behind the cat eye specs. Her looks don't matter. How she makes you feel does. And making you feel is what she does *best*.

POSSIBLE OUTCOME

Oh this is luscious and heady stuff. A very sexy, romantic time is in store. Downsides are few, but as always, keep your head! This is an exciting partner in crime. Enjoy!

KING OF CUPS

TRADITIONAL MEANING

Charming, intelligent and creative man. Romantic person. Gracious and kind. Poets, artists and writers.

ROMANCE READING

What happens to the bad boy when he's all grown up? Usually they go one of two ways. They either never grow up and slowly stagnate and eventually degenerate into middle aged lotharios who wonder why they just don't quite draw the crowd they used to, and are reduced to being a seductive but ultimately disappointing episode in a number of women's lives, or, they smarten up and become a pretty tasty catch.

The best and worst of the King of Cups is revealed in these two outcomes, but let's assume the best, shall we? We can spot a playboy easily, because we are savvy and sharp, and so know to avoid them easily. Right?...*Right?*

So, on the plus side we have a very, very charming, attractive, creative, sensitive creature who might finally, *finally* be ready to settle down. The nice part is that when he does choose to do this, The King of Cups is a marvelous partner indeed: devoted, romantic, and loyal. Just watch out. Your friends will still flirt with him and he might flirt right back. Harmlessly. Be of secure stuff.

The best way to keep the King of Cups happy is to make him feel desired, attractive and appreciated. Notice the little things he does for you, and he will reward you with devotion.

POSSIBLE OUTCOME

Hey, Girl. Looks like you have landed Mr. Dreamy McDreamboat. Way to go. Just make sure he isn't a Colin Ferrell in a Ryan Gosling costume.

THE SUIT OF SWORDS

Image copyright J. Daniels with elements used with permission.

Okay. There is really no way to spin this. The Swords in love are melancholy indeed. Other than the clean cutting and fervent Ace, and the brilliant and intellectual Court Cards, the moody and dark Swords are always less than welcome in a romance spread.

All is not lost, though. Forewarned is often forearmed, and sometimes knowing the pricklier aspects of a situation is a marvelous way to side step it entirely!

ACE OF SWORDS

TRADITIONAL MEANING

"Cutting through the dross". Surgery. Truth spoken bluntly. Honestly. Swift change. Strength.

ROMANCE READING

Blunt speaking does have a place in romance. Yes, sweet nothings and ardent compliments are to be treasured and savored, but there are moments when shiny, bright truth is needed. This is where the Ace of Swords comes in.

On the plus side, The Ace of Swords very often represents PASSION. Like the Ace of Wands, this Ace is a phallic symbol, though with, quite literally, an edge.

On the more challenging side, need to have a talk? This is the moment when feelings previously hidden come to the surface with force and everyone soon comes to know where they stand. When this card appears, know you are getting the truth, even if it stings a little. After the confrontation promised by the Ace is over, the air will be clear. This can only be good, no?

POSSIBLE OUTCOME

Hot stuff. Serious infatuation. Strong lust. Look for these exciting feelings to come your way… *at least in the mind.* This is an interesting aspect that can be found in this suit in general. While the Cups are all heart, the Swords are pure intellect. Without other suit cards to propel these feelings into real world action, they might remain only thoughts, played with as a mental exercise.

Remember: Words are not deeds.

TWO OF SWORDS

TRADITIONAL MEANING

Truce. Stalemate. Temporary peace. Can mean balance in a difficult situation.

ROMANCE READING

There is just no way around this, Star Pirate. This card is a bummer in a love reading, straight up.

The Two of Swords in a love reading is love offered… and rejected. When you have found yourself in love with an emotionally unavailable or avoidant type, or if you find yourself acting out in this way, this card will often turn up in a reading.

This is especially painful if your romance started out ardent and warm. Why the change? *Why can't they be like they were in the beginning?* Some people just have a short shelf life. They can only handle so much closeness before panic and pulling back sets in. This can be particularly cruel in that this panic tends to show up when things would naturally become deeper in expression, such as after sex, or a particularly great date, or a wonderful weekend together.

Painful stuff.

Maybe it is YOU who is panicking? Be aware of how painful that can feel to be on the receiving end of that. Maybe it's time to feel the fear…and show up anyway? The rewards can be great, in spite of how vulnerable and scary the intimacy can feel. Only you know how ready you are for love, so just be careful not to use someone else for emotional support, sex, ego strokes, and other goodies while you figure it out.

On a gentler note, as is often the case in an otherwise very positive reading, this card can sometimes show up when one of you simply needs some space.

I know. I know. Feels pretty miserable when mutual energy shifts into what feels like a pursuit and avoidance dynamic, but everyone needs time to do their own thing, and it's good to *give the gift of letting someone miss you*. You know what to do, right? Pull back, let go, focus on friends, hobbies, interests, and truly know that this other person is NOT your Moon and Stars, and you have a rich full life without them. Don't ask about it, just let go and do your own thing. And yes, this means seeing other people, if you can.

Very often this rather quickly results in the return of the beloved…but…

POSSIBLE OUTCOME

…sometimes it doesn't. The Two of Swords in this position suggests the emotional unavailability of your romantic partner will grow more apparent over time.

Just know in your heart that "winning over" the one who is "hard to catch" isn't really a testimony of your value and lovability. You are absolutely lovable right now. You deserve someone warm and open and really, really into you, so don't settle for Mr. or Ms. Unavailable.

So. Do your life, spend time with people who love you, and remember that your newly limp lover is not the only person who will ever make your heart thump.

THREE OF SWORDS

TRADITIONAL MEANING

Painful Revelation. Heartbreak. Loss. Melodrama.

ROMANCE READING

While the Three of Swords looks like the Worst Card EVER, it's actually not *that bad*. Ok, it's *bad*, but it's not the worst. The Three of Swords is the epitome of "sound and fury, signifying nothing".

What do I mean by this? I mean that yes, it is a card that can signify a breakup, but one that feels intensely painful at the beginning, but from which you rather surprisingly and quickly recover. That perfect person you thought would be the great love of your life? Meh! A few weeks later you realize this one is actually sort of a weenie, and hey, look at that cutie over there!

The Three of Swords can also mean that you are blindsided by upsetting news, such as finding out your romantic interest is actually married, or a drug user, or has an upsetting criminal record.

Regardless, the worst has passed. Even if in the future position, this is a card of hot, fast pain, shocking and over quickly. You will survive.

POSSIBLE OUTCOME

Bad spot for this one, I'm sorry to say. Try, if you can, to sidestep or prevent a blow up of an argument, a painful surprise, or a mean and callous little breakup. The nice news is, again, as painful as it might feel, you will right yourself quickly like the cool cucumber you are, because you are well rid of that experience.

FOUR OF SWORDS

TRADITIONAL MEANING

Rest, repose, and a break in the midst of battle.

ROMANCE READING

Two possible meanings here, depending on the cards that surround Four of Swords, as well as the Querent's specific circumstances. The Four of Swords more commonly can be a simple expression of emotional and physical rest and withdrawal. Time to yourself, a break from dating, an emotional retreat. Love is easy; dating can be hard.

There is another aspect to this card, though, that can be important. This card represents someone who is emotionally shut down. This could be an emotionally unavailable partner, who is cool in tone and lacking tenderness, or it can mean that being in an emotionally, or, heaven forbid, physically volatile relationship has caused one of you to shut down emotionally in an attempt to protect the self.

If this is the case, rest is not what is needed; action is your next move. By action, I mean the swift removal of yourself from this toxic situation. Please take very good care.

POSSIBLE OUTCOME

Assuming all is well otherwise, you need some downtime and possibly alone time. Sometimes in the quest to find love it is good to take a break, and it looks like this is the moment for that. Rest a bit and refresh yourself, so you can jump into the fray again!

FIVE OF SWORDS

TRADITIONAL MEANING

Conflict and stress. Fighting dirty. Winning at the great cost of reduced respect from others.

ROMANCE READING

Ugh. This is ugly fighting. Mean and selfish. This is the kind of fighting a certain type of person *actually enjoys*. This is bringing a cannon to a knife fight.

There are people in the world who simply can't stand a win/win outcome. Someone needs to lose, and it must be the other person, even to the point of being willing to take oneself down with the ship to achieve that dark victory.

Be very careful here. This is very toxic behavior, and the type of person who desires to "win" at all costs is someone that can cause permanent damage to both their victims and certainly the relationship.

Sounds pretty grim, eh? I won't kid around here: I hate this card. Sure, it might show up as just a snarly little exchange, but pay attention. Someone who is entirely willing to cause deliberate damage with words is someone you don't want to press to your heart.

If YOU are the "win at all costs" fighter here…please become aware of your deep need to damage in order to suppress and conquer. You might get over what you said in the imagined heat of battle, but I promise you that your victim is still shaking, *and they WILL remember*.

POSSIBLE OUTCOME

BAD. The outcome is one of suppression, manipulation, and toxic behavior. If it's one nasty, mean little fight, work hard to communicate better than you have been, and maybe you can both quit treating the other like an adversary. If not, please consider this a bad fit and move on.

Remember: misery really and truly has no place in love and partnership. It does not make it more passionate or "real". It simply makes it heartbreaking.

SIX OF SWORDS

TRADITIONAL READING

Travel near water. Moving to a safe place. Escape.

ROMANCE READING

The Six of Swords is a tiny island of calm in the sea of sharks that are the Swords.

This serene card is a representation of blue skies after a storm, or a moving towards a safer, quieter space. It can even mean a literal move to a new home.

This can manifest in a number of ways. It might mean that you find that the break up of your relationship turns out to be a very lovely thing, because you soon realize how unhappy you were, and now you are open to something much sweeter that is now coming your way. Wonderful. Way to take care of yourself!

OR, it can mean that in an existing relationship, you finally decide that both of you are doing this all wrong, and you are committed to the slow deliberate growth that comes with changing hurtful behavior. Maybe you both go into counseling and learn a different style of communication. Maybe you resolve to change how you handle money problems or allocate housework. Maybe you simply decide to let go of a problem that is more about having control over another rather than actual resolution.

There are some problems that have no solution. You can choose to accept and live in peace with that. The adage, "Would you rather be 'right' or happy?" really applies here.

POSSIBLE OUTCOME

In this position it is strongly suggested that a stormy time in your life is now passing and you are moving to a much more tranquil and pleasant place. Thank goodness. More of this, please!

SEVEN OF SWORDS

TRADITIONAL MEANING

Deception, manipulation, and playing both sides to achieve an outcome. Cleverness wins.

ROMANCE READING

Tricky card, the Seven of Swords. In spite of the fact that it traditionally means what you see above, it can also have a somewhat positive meaning as well, which I will get to in a moment.

This is the card of duplicity. By this I mean that it is a card of using deception, in word or deed, to turn the tide in your favor and win the outcome of your choice. In business, this can be an excellent thing, and sometimes needed in a cutthroat world.

But in love, honesty and transparency create the path to warm intimacy, so it is a weapon that needs to be wielded with skill and caution.

In the beginning of a romance, this can mean the "best self" you present to your potential partner while you are wooing each other. That is normal and to be expected. It is the clever convincing you do when you are trying to win the heart of another.

But, be careful. It can also mean that your potential romance or even existing partner is not being entirely honest with you. This is ALSO the card of infidelity, so if you are concerned that all is not what it seems to be, pay close attention!

So, even when you are acting with noble and ultimately sincere intentions, make sure there comes a time when you drop the pretense and show your real self. You need to know that you can be loved for who you truly are, because this "Cool Girl" or "Prince Perfect" is an act you can't keep up forever.

POSSIBLE OUTCOME

Time to pay closer attention to what is happening in your romance. The Seven of Swords in this position suggests deception in the future. NO, this does not mean it's ok to look at their phone or email, suspicious and searching, but it's certainly time to have a chat. So have one!

EIGHT OF SWORDS

TRADITIONAL MEANING

Self imposed restriction. Feeling stuck. Learned helplessness.

ROMANCE READING

In a traditional tarot deck, the striking Eight of Swords usually depicts a woman, blindfolded, arms bound, in the middle of a circle of swords. She looks helpless and trapped in her tiny prison, but if you look again, you will notice that all is not as it seems.

That blindfold is about to come loose. Those binds around her arms are loosely tied, and the swords that encircle her like a corral are loosely spaced and once she shakes off her bonds with ease, she might easily walk between those sharp edges to freedom.

So why doesn't she?

Sometimes we feel trapped in relationships, almost as if we have to stay. Yes, in well-established marriages with children, this can seem very true, but even then, you have choices.

For most of us, it's just a crappy relationship that is going nowhere, or a crappy relationship in a shared living space that feels impossible to leave, and this type of trapped thinking is a mistake, and it comes from a feeling of scarcity…of feeling like this is all there is, and the best you can do, so let's make the most of it.

Scarcity thinking is especially bad for new relationships, as it can cause you to commit to someone who is far less than ideal simply because you feel like you either can't "do any better," or worse, DESERVE any better, and so you settle, and you settle hard.

I want to make it clear here that I am not at all advocating for flighty fickleness and an endless "I can always trade up" mentality. That is also a barrier to intimacy and love. There is everything to be said for making a commitment strong enough that you feel emotionally safe and sticking to it. The idea that "we are in this space together, and no one is going anywhere, so let's work it out" is great, and to be encouraged, but there is another side to this that you want to avoid, and that is committing to a sucky someone because you have "invested so much."

Don't let your "sunk costs" be your prison. There is such a thing as misplaced loyalty.

Look carefully at your prison bars, and shake the door. It might already be open.

POSSIBLE OUTCOME

Someone is feeling very trapped, even if they are free. Time to see if that can be fixed, or if you need to take off the blindfold and run!

NINE OF SWORDS

TRADITIONAL MEANING

Dark night of the soul. Shame and worry. Fear of catastrophe.

ROMANCE READING

Wow, Star Pirate-Lover Person, I pondered how to approach this card, because this and the one that follows are probably the most troublesome cards in the deck, and I can't have you feeling brokenhearted without at least some glimmer of hope.

Firstly, all tarot readings are to be considered as a guideline for what could happen if you continue on the current course. There is nothing set in stone. You can change an outcome, or at least *your part* in an outcome, and this is relevant here.

Secondly, well, let's get to that.

The Nine of Swords is the 3am toss and turn in bed, deeply fretful that you are about to be exposed in a shameful or horrible situation. It is the fear that you have done something so *stupid* and you are about to get *caught* and it's *too late now* and everything is going to turn into a poop sandwich.

The good news is that with the Nine of Swords, the "world-shattering catastrophe" is most likely all in your head, and if there are bad outcomes to be had in the real world, they are most likely smaller potatoes than you suppose. Nowhere near the disaster you imagine. This is especially true if very positive cards are in the same spread, such as The Sun, The World, or the Nine of Pentacles or any of the Aces. In fact, if the Sun appears in a spread with this card…your worry is for no reason at all. Please stop torturing yourself!

The element of shame is an important aspect to this card, and you should pay attention to it. If you have done something you consider shameful, it's time to right the situation as soon as possible. There is every chance you will "get away with it" so to speak, but that doesn't make your mistake any less, um, mistakey. Shame is very toxic because, unlike guilt, it's not about disappointment in what you have done; it's disappointment in *who you are*. That's no good, and rarely appropriate…as in, never.

So either fix it, or make with the self-compassion, pronto!

POSSIBLE OUTCOME

Someone is terrified of getting in big trouble. Someone is fearful that they have done a Very Bad Thing. Hopefully it will vanish like a nightmare in the morning light, but otherwise, definitely get on that before it explodes!

If you think this card might be about how your romantic interest feels about you, rather than your feelings about yourself, then I am sorry. This tends to mean that the other person feels so stressed by you and your relationship that they are avoiding all contact, feeling guilty about it, and are being generally avoidant. It's a childish response, but a common one, and again, a good time to take very good care of yourself. Pull way back, and spend time with people who love you.

TEN OF SWORDS

TRADITIONAL MEANING

Cruelty. Crushing defeat. Worst is over. Total collapse.

ROMANCE READING

Let's just put the kettle on straight away, before we go on, ok?

The ideal place for this sorrowful card is in the past position of a spread. Even the present position is fine, because you will already be in pain and know what is causing this to happen.

Alas, the future is just a crummy place for this to show up. This is a card of absolute endings, cruel behavior, and yes, defeat, but there is good reason not to utterly despair.

In a traditional tarot card, a man, grey in death, lies on the ground with ten swords stuck in his back...but look beyond this grim scene. In the background is a sunrise, and it is there purposefully to tell you the worst is over, or very soon to be, and this is not forever.

Yes, this does suggest that someone will let you down in a spectacular sort of way, but it will not kill you.

An otherwise positive spread will surely mitigate the pain represented here, but there is definitely pain to be had. You might just get dumped, and it's painful and hard and you will feel a bit crushed, but not for long, and it doesn't mean you will never love again. That sunrise promises just that, so take heart, lover.

POSSIBLE OUTCOME

I fear that if there were ever a card that said "…and they didn't live happily ever after," it would be this one, so in an outcome card position the Ten of Swords suggests an ending. I tend to believe things don't work out for a reason, so you might find in hindsight this was a blessing. Sometimes people we imagine we want the most are directly in front of the one we are truly meant to be with, so consider this one more obstacle removed on your journey to love.

Regardless, and again, take very good care of yourself, and know you are entirely lovable, even if it is not happening right at this very moment.

PAGE OF SWORDS

TRADITIONAL MEANING

Younger, intellectual person. Cerebral communication. Cool personality

ROMANCE READING

As a person, our Page is one of cool disposition, even lacking in passion. This is someone who lives in his or her head, and feels perfectly fine with that…thank you very much! Highly intelligent and a fun person with whom to have long talks late into the night, this young man or woman is not really of a romantic bent.

You might find your Page frustrating, especially if you crush on a big brain. They might be a bit clueless in matters of the heart. This person will make an excellent friend, but possibly a bad romantic partner. I'm not saying that they are asexual. I am saying though, that sex might be their only way of expressing tenderness or affection, so if you are looking for affectionate warmth outside of the bedroom, said Page might not be for you.

As a situation, this can mean something as simple as an intense conversation that changes things in your relationship, or a cool reception to your romantic overtures. Not necessarily a bad thing, but if you are looking for fire, expect instead cool steel.

POSSIBLE OUTCOME

Most likely just a conversation that clears the air. Expect very straight talk soon.

THE KNIGHT OF SWORDS

TRADITIONAL MEANING:

Unpredictable and wild young man. Information given in a tactless manner.

ROMANCE READING

Oh look, it's Danger Boy. Sigh. Handsome and charming and devil-may-care, here is the one that will sweep you off your feet and then drop you as soon as you start to get used to all the heady deliciousness of it all.

The sexy, but emotionally distant man that you want to "win", because he is a challenge? This guy.

The man who gets recruited for the CIA? This guy.

Is that a promise? No. There are exceptions to this. Sometimes the Knight of Swords means there is a smart, intense, and sexy guy is in your life, and he doesn't suffer fools lightly. Can you match that energy? Then he might be your guy, and you two can be the intense couple in all black that hangs out in the corner at parties and wonders how long they have to make small talk before they can go home.

Otherwise, you might find him a bit…frosty, if great in the sack.

POSSIBLE OUTCOME

WHOOSH. What just happened? Did you get swept up in something that feels out of your control? Hold on to your knickers. Things might be getting very exciting, very soon.

QUEEN OF SWORDS

TRADITIONAL MEANING

Intelligent, passionate woman. Straight talk. Good friend. Elegant wife.

ROMANCE READING

Ever been called a bitch by a man…because you disagreed with him?

Ever been called...intimidating?
Are you, shall we say, a bit blunt with your thoughts?
Then you understand this queen. What others don't know is this: She loves fiercely and strongly and would kick the butt of anyone who messed with the friend she *just chewed out* for going out on a date with YET ANOTHER unemployed musician.

The Queen has intellect and drive and puts up with very little stupid. And, underneath all that beats a passionate and tender heart, indeed.

This is the Queen of Swords personified. She seems rather tough on the outside, and she is, but she is a powerful, good-hearted, deeply loyal friend and partner, and would make any man an excellent, elegant wife. Or partner in crime.

…He had better have a strong sense of self, though. Domineering, smothering, indecisive or unambitious men need not apply.

She is traditionally depicted as a redhead or a brunette, but this is, again, a traditional depiction, and should not be taken as a must in any way.

POSSIBLE OUTCOME

The Queen will choose the right thing. By right thing, I mean she chooses what is best for herself. Everyone else will just have to deal with it.

KING OF SWORDS

TRADITIONAL MEANING

Strong, intellectual man. Critical thinking. Critical words. Cool head.

ROMANCE READING

Danger! Danger! Danger!

Ok, maybe not DANGER, but…um, danger. Here's why:

King of Swords? Sexy. Super, duper sexy. Highly intelligent, well groomed, good in business, very, very competent. James Bond is the King of Swords personified, at least at first blush, so you see where I am going here.

Attracted to the emotionally remote? Why, you can have it in spades, with this guy! Yes, yes, he is super hot, and maybe you can win his heart, but really, his heart belongs to Daddy…and he's Daddy. Always. Also, be prepared for lots of unsolicited criticism about, well, everything. Do not ask him if you look fat in that dress *unless you really want to know*.

Is your self-esteem so shaky that only "capturing" the one hardest to capture will do? He's your guy!

The upside? If he truly loves you, boy, he loves you, but you had best bring your A-game.

I find it rather exhausting, myself.

POSSIBLE OUTCOME

Expect some criticism to come your way. Whether it is justified, fair, or true is up to you. Think carefully, and don't let someone else dim your shine!

THE SUIT OF PENTACLES

Image copyright J. Daniels: elements used with permission.

The Pentacles (sometimes called the Coins) are eminently practical, and are often concerned with work and money. They also most certainly have a role to play in romance readings. For example, they are marvelous boosters and grounders! They make the nice cards nicer and the flaky cards stronger and more stable, and that is a marvelous thing! Also, one should never discount the role money plays in a relationship. The lack of it can cause a great deal of stress, and a great deal of it can affect the dynamic of a relationship if there is an imbalance of power between the Have and the Have Not.

ACE OF PENTACLES

TRADITIONAL MEANING

New business venture, the start of a new undertaking that is prosperous. Wealth.

ROMANCE READING

I really like the Ace of Pentacles a lot.

It's a very friendly card indeed, and while all the Aces have a nice effect on a reading (generally making it more positive and mitigating the negative cards in a spread), I find that the Ace of Pentacles is the most powerful of the Aces for this. This card tamps down the negatives for even Big Bads like the Tower, or the Nine of Swords, and can sometimes reduce them to mere unpleasant little moments. In a romance spread, the Ace of this suit symbolizes plenty, abundance and the freedom that financial security brings to a romance. It could be that your suitor is prosperous, and that you will have luxe adventures together. This is especially true if the World, the Empress or The Emperor is present. Just watch out for the Emperor, as he can be very controlling with his combination of power, entitlement and money.

If you are looking for an old school provider and protector, well, he's your guy, but remember there are downsides to that kind of control.

Watch out also if this card is paired with The Devil. Money seduces and excess is easy with this combination. Brace yourself for the hangover, if you overindulge.

POSSIBLE OUTCOME

This is a brilliant card to have as an outcome card. Happy days are here again! Whatever your concern, there is a new, prosperous, and sensual change of circumstance about to take place.

TWO OF PENTACLES

TRADITIONAL MEANING

Borrowing from Peter to pay Paul. Low on funds but light of heart. Juggling work life and home life

ROMANCE READING

This card concerns itself with everyday life, so when it appears in a romance spread you have a few ways to interpret it that are perfectly legit, depending on the querant's circumstances.

In one scenario, this means that things have gotten a little stale. NOT BAD, I want to be clear, but things possibly have become routine and comfortable and that is both nice…and dangerous. Not only is variety the spice of life, but doing things that are even a tiny bit new together, like trying a new restaurant or even playing a new game or having a tiny adventure, can strengthen and deepen a bond between couples. Try it and see if you don't look at your sweetie with fresh eyes.

Or, in another interpretation of the Two of Pentacles, you might be at a crossroads in the relationship and a choice will be made soon. Do you move in together? Maybe get engaged? This card is a minor, rather than loud and colorful, indication of this happening in the near future. It might not be the Big Proposal, but certainly someone is thinking about upping the ante in your romance.

POSSIBLE OUTCOME

Look for a decision to be made regarding your relationship. As this is not a negative card, it will be a positive outcome, but maybe not momentous...yet.

THREE OF PENTACLES

TRADITIONAL MEANING

Moving from Journeyman to Master. Coming together to create something important. Commitment.

ROMANTIC READING

Context is king with the Three of Pentacles, but in all romantic permutations it is positive. This is a card sharply affected by the other cards in the spread, but it does stand alone as a positive card, suggesting that a new level of commitment is in the works for your relationship.

For a person already in a relationship, when this card appears in a spread with the Usual Suspects of Big Romance (Lovers, Two and Ten of Cups, The Star, The Sun), there might be an engagement or proposal coming within the next year.

For a person who is single and dating, the Three of Pentacles suggests that more than one quality person is out there for you, so take heart!

For a person in a difficult relationship, this card can sometimes mean that there is a third person, waiting in the wings, should this relationship collapse. This is doubly so should the Seven of Swords (clever duplicity wins the game!) or the charming and seductive Magician appear in the spread.

POSSIBLE OUTCOME

Everything written about this card above is enhanced in an outcome position. Be sure to look at other cards in the spread to see which way the wind blows.

FOUR OF PENTACLES

TRADITIONAL MEANING

Miserly behavior. Valuing possessions over experiences or people.

ROMANCE READING

Have you ever dated someone who seemed very charming at first, but rather quickly devolved into this new and heartbreaking person who is emotionally stingy, not particularly affectionate, obviously afraid of intimacy, and highly protective of their space? Someone who, for some reason, stuck around in your life, assuring your mutual unhappiness until you finally end it in a tearful tornado of frustration and bewilderment? (whew!)

You have had a Four of Pentacles Experience!

This card is a clear cut representation of the Emotionally Avoidant attachment style, and people of this orientation can only handle small amounts of intimacy before a very powerful and fearful need to control the space between you kicks in, leaving you feeling confused and lonely. These are not bad people, but they won't be able to come around easily. You can't love them "better".

Watch out for someone who engages in little cruelties in order to upset you and confirm their unconscious belief that romance is more trouble than it is worth. Painful stuff.

Look for any of the following cards to confirm this: the Five of Swords (fighting for funsies!), the Eight of Swords (a prison of your own making, but one from which you can easily escape), the Two of Swords (emotional withdrawal/unavailability, rejection of love), and The Hermit (a desire to be alone and control your environment).

On the other side of the coin, and depending on where this card falls in a spread, it can mean that you are feeling possessive in a way that is focused more on "acquiring" the person you want, in an almost objectifying way, rather than truly caring for them.

The Emperor landing in a spread along with this card is strong affirmation of this tendency to objectify.

Finally and again, as with most Pentacles, context is so important. This card might represent a less complex but equally vexing issue, such as who controls the purse strings in your relationship? Is money a source of friction between you? Time to talk about it before it festers!

Careful discernment and self-awareness is needed to interpret this card correctly. Keep an open mind regarding your own behavior!

POSSIBLE OUTCOME

As an outcome card, this does suggest the object of your affection is emotionally remote, and focused on things other than you. It is maddening to see someone who was once warm and charming slowly back out the door, figuratively or literally! If you see it happening, try to let them go. No amount of careful behavior on your part is going to fix this. It's really not you.

….unless it is. Again, watch for possessiveness and attempts to control others purely to calm your own fears.

FIVE OF PENTACLES

TRADITIONAL MEANING

Sadness. Loneliness. Financial instability. Business failure. Feeling left out.

ROMANCE READING

Oh dear!

Here's the good news, Star Pirate: Tarot speaks in big bold symbols, and the extreme representations of misery on the cards often only manifest as dainty poop sandwiches you have to nibble on a bit, and then toss.

Here's the bad news: There's a dainty poop sandwich in your future.

Or at least, there might be, if you don't take things in hand right away. This IS traditionally a card of breakup. I won't mince words here. This is a classic card of being Separated From What You Want Very Much. ...BUT...

Sometimes this is just a miserable fight that nearly ends your relationship. You recover, but it takes a while.

Sometimes it means your partner loses a job and is terrified and miserable, so please be gentle and try not to fan their freak-out flames with your own fears.

Sometimes it means you are having an extreme emotional reaction to something that is actually not all that dire. Perspective is needed.

A traditional illustration of this card always shows a ragged, freezing family outside a beautiful home whose light filled windows show a scene of a table groaning with abundant food, cheer and warmth, and this might be just how you feel right now: like everyone is having a great time but you, and you will never, ever be happy again.

Look for positive cards in the spread to mitigate this. If The World is in the spread, it means that this pain you feel now is only the ending of a miserable phase of your life, and you are on to bigger and better things! If the Sun appears, it means you come upon a revealed truth that makes staying in the relationship impossible, but thank goodness you know!

If Death appears, well, it's over. I mean really over. The bandage was ripped off on the count of "one." This is doubly so if the Tower appears, and it is entirely out of your control, and not your fault.

Other Five cards in the spread add to the punch of Pentacles, especially the Five of Cups. Fives are bummers in Tarot, generally, but the least of them is the Wands. If the Five of Wands appears with this card, you have a good chance of fighting your way back to a good place, if you keep a cool head.

If the Big Daddy of "Fives" appears in a spread as well, The Heriophant (Major Arcana #5), it means that adopting a very reserved, traditional, calm and classy demeanor will go a long way towards softening the effects of this card.

No matter what happens, how you feel now is not how you will feel forever.

POSSIBLE OUTCOME

This is where loss is especially likely. I hope it's only a tiny bite of that sandwich.

SIX OF PENTACLES

TRADITIONAL MEANING

Generosity, philanthropy, charity. Taking care of others. Financial success. Fairness

ROMANCE READING

This is a very straightforward card, and the interpretation of it is either positive or less than positive depending on which way the wind is blowing with respect to the other cards in the spread.

Fairness and balance in a relationship are the main themes of this card, so often and most likely the Six of Pentacles just states that in this relationship both of you have a strong sense of fairness, balance and generosity. You care that each other's needs are well met. Both of you contribute equally to the relationship, with the knowledge that giving even more than just 50% makes it all work.

The only time this card is unfavorable is when negative cards are present as a majority in the spread. Then this card suggests a "one down" position for someone in the relationship, through money, power or control.

If this is a new relationship, be sure that everyone is on a place of equal footing.

POSSIBLE OUTCOME

Having this card in the outcome position is favorable! This suggests fairness and material comfort is to be had in this relationship. Even more importantly, you are both on the same page with regard to your needs, wants and hopes for the future. Good stuff!

SEVEN OF PENTACLES

TRADITIONAL MEANING

Efforts made will reap rewards. Pausing to reflect.

ROMANCE READING

There is a famous example of psychological bias called The Sunk Costs Fallacy. This is normally about business, but it can easily apply to relationships as well. It boils down to this: We often stick with someone despite all signs pointing to a poor fit. We stay because we have poured effort and energy into this romance, dating is so dang hard, and leaving now feels like quitting too soon. We have already invested so much, we think we are so close, but basically we *perceive* the relationship has greater value than it objectively does.

In fact, this is such an effective bias that we often throw "good money after bad" in an effort to salvage past choices. Rarely a good idea!

The Seven of Pentacles is here to help you step back, breathe, and assess. It's a pause to refresh, as it were.

In this card a young man is looking rather melancholy, and is leaning on his hoe, gazing upon a garden rich with pentacle coins. Now is the moment right before harvest, and things look good.

Why the long face, then? He is deciding if the work was worth the reward.

You might soon be at a tipping point where you decide if this relationship is one worthy of deeper investment. The cards around it, and of course, your personal experience, will answer that.

There is nothing wrong at all with pulling back a bit and assessing the value and possible future of your romance before you sink any more of yourself, your time, effort and money into it. The opportunity to do that is soon upon you.

Just because you invested time and effort and love into something doesn't mean it can give you back what you need. Look carefully at the situation you are in, and take heart...there is nothing negative about this card, as you will either realize you are happy and wanting to go forward, or that you need to take your ball and go home.

For a single person, it's the moment before you sign up for a dating site, or go to that party. In this instance I would encourage the investment, as it could pay off big!

POSSIBLE OUTCOME

Decision time! Take some time and look at this relationship. Could be a tipping point of commitment!

EIGHT OF PENTACLES

TRADITIONAL MEANING

Hard work and dedication. Doing what needs to be done. Small gains over time.

ROMANCE READING

I know what you are thinking. Ho Hum. Not a very romantic card. A man at a bench, hammering out pentacle stamped shields. Laborious work, and he currently looks none too prosperous.

Looks can be deceiving!

I think the Eight of Pentacles is one of the most romantic of the Pentacle cards, and here's why:

The Eight of Pentacles is a card of loyalty and commitment. This card represents a person who is going to stay and work hard to make a relationship stable and happy. He or she is the person who is loyal through the tough times, willing to go to therapy to learn how to communicate better, and generally shows up like a grown up. He's a mensch, and She's a devoted, kind hearted, emotionally intelligent soul.

This is not a flighty person. In a world that increasingly values non-committal "chill" over earnest expressions of intent, desire and devotion -- this is very romantic indeed!

The only drawback to this card is that it can represent someone who might be loyal to someone unworthy of this kind of care. Make sure everyone involved is equally noble of intent!

POSSIBLE OUTCOME

Everyone involved intends to stick it out through the hard times. Small gains, over time, reap romantic rewards and increased bonding and connection. It can also mean small financial gains and comforts over time that make your life together easier. This is a sweet little card that should make you smile when it lands in this position. Just make sure that other negative cards in the spread don't point to misplaced loyalty!

NINE OF PENTACLES

TRADITIONAL MEANING

Luxury, comfort, being free of care. Alone in luxury.

ROMANCE READING

A lovely card on its own, the Nine of Pentacles is about security, luxury and comfort. Nothing wrong with that at all. This card, though, also tends to mean that you enjoy this luxury alone.

It could be that your desire for emotional space and comfort and security means you hold people at arm's length as a form of self-protection, or that your romantic interest does this to you.

This is not a card of deep feeling. There could be a shallowness to the company you share. There is no emotional ugliness to this card, but that is because there is little in the way of deep emotion present at all.

If this card is in a position that represents the other person in your life, beware of the seductive delights of nice dating experiences and the traditional trappings of romance rather than a more genuine and soulful connection. It might surprise you that all these grand gestures don't mean much to the person dazzling you with adventure.

POSSIBLE OUTCOME

Alors...style over substance! It will be fun for a while, and you might enjoy some nice little adventures together, but don't expect high romance. It's just not likely to be found here.
Or -- maybe that is just what you need right now?

TEN OF PENTACLES

TRADITIONAL MEANING

Wealth. Inheritance. Material comfort.

ROMANCE READING

There is a lot to be said for material comfort. Takes a great deal of stress away from day-to-day life, and that can be wonderful. Studies suggest most fights between couples are money stress related. Evidence of deeply secure comfort is depicted in the Ten of Pentacles, and it does suggest that becoming part of a wealthy family, or receiving an inheritance, could be in your future.

What this card does not promise, though, is emotional happiness. It's not a negative card at all, but one of the central meanings of this card is "luxury and comfort can sometimes mean boredom rather than happiness." While it is hard to imagine this being true as you struggle to pay the bills, there are plenty of famous people in the world who can confirm the fact that all the material comfort one can imagine does not assure happiness.

Now, having said that…all this goes out the window in a spread that has one or more of these: Ace of Cups, Two of Cups, Lovers, or the Emperor and Empress together in a spread…then, whoa! Fairy tale stuff, either on a grand scale, or a smaller, sweeter and more manageable scale, is possible here.

Very Happily Ever After. Good Luck!

POSSIBLE OUTCOME

The same meaning as an outcome card as stated above! Look for romance cards to be included in the spread to assume emotional happiness. Watch out for negative cards that suggest a comfortable but cold partnership.

PAGE OF PENTACLES

TRADITIONAL MEANING

Thoughtful young person. Well off. Intelligent and practical. Careful focus and discernment.

ROMANCE READING

The young person depicted in the Page of Pentacles is as smart and practical as they come. All the Pages have their defining romantic characteristics: Wands are emotional passion, Cups are love, Swords intellectual connection…and the Pentacles are about sex! Surprising, I know, but by sex I don't mean the sweeping, loving, passionate kind found in the other suits. I mean the "sex is fun, so let's do it" sort of casual encounter that can be fun, but lacking in deeper connection.

Also, watch out. This Page is smart but less emotionally invested than most, and can easily walk away from situations others might cling to.

This is not a bad person (unless other cards around him confirm that idea). This is just a person who enjoys things on a simple, material level, rather than a soulful or heartfelt one.

OUTCOME

A wait and see outcome. Pages are "New Relationships"…new romances. So now is the time to observe and enjoy, rather than decide or attempt to control.

He might be a nice, handsome, practical guy you enjoy as a friend with benefits. Or, you might wonder why this guy seems like such a catch on paper, but is such a false start in person. Observe!

KNIGHT OF PENTACLES

TRADITIONAL MEANING

Calm person. Well off man. Devoted Man. Earthy person. Constancy.

ROMANCE READING

Ahh.

This is where we meet the first of the three most gracious, committed in love, generous and warmly open "people" in Tarot.

In a traditional Tarot deck, the Knight of Pentacles is the only knight that isn't galloping, running, bucking or otherwise being ADVENTURE BOY.

He is instead fancily dressed in dark dress armor, sitting calmly on a large, black, gorgeous horse that is well groomed and standing still. Grapes and vines are a motif for the Pentacles and are all around him, symbolizing wine, pleasure, and wealth.

If you are looking for a passionate, committed, ardent, and most of all STEADFAST partner in love, you really can't go wrong here. If there is a downside to this knight, it may be that people who need constant variety and excitement might find him a little dull. These are also people who find actual intimacy a daunting thing to be avoided. Let them go off and have their doomed romances. This Knight is here to stay, and will say so.

Bonus: he is a thoughtful and attentive lover.

Good times.

POSSIBLE OUTCOME

SCORE! Fist bump. What a catch! Your mother will be terribly pleased! Even as a circumstance this card stands for calm, tranquil, secure abundance. Nice!

QUEEN OF PENTACLES

TRADITIONAL MEANING

Gracious, generous host. Beautiful home and thoughtful care. A kind and loving woman.

ROMANCE READING

The Queen of Pentacles is the epitome of someone who in the past might have been referred to as a Very Classy Broad.

And she is. The man who has her in his life is a lucky, lucky man. She is warm and kind and sensual and creates beautiful homes and is emotionally and materially generous to a fault. She is a nurturer and a giver and a cook and a homemaker supreme (when not possibly running her own law firm!).

Our Queen of Pentacles doesn't do well with poverty, though. She will be gracious and kind even in struggle but, seriously, she needs her comforts. Like the Empress, a starving artist's life is not for her. Having said that, of course, when she visits starving artists she brings homemade lasagna and wine and good cheer.

All the good qualities she possesses stand as a definition of this card, even when there is no "person" connected to it. See it abstractly then, as a circumstance. Look for kindness and comfort. This is an island of calm in a turbulent world.

POSSIBLE OUTCOME

Same as above, only more so!

For a man's reading, it is entirely possible you have found THE ONE FOR YOU, of either gender.

KING OF PENTACLES

TRADITIONAL MEANING

Wealthy, earthy, practical man. Generous.

ROMANTIC READING

Everyone has his or her type, and everyone has his or her needs, but the King of Pentacles is, in many ways, as close as one gets to someone with a fairly universal appeal, simply because he is very kind, calm, prosperous, generous, warm, and very good hearted.

Is he an intellectual? He's not stupid by a long shot, but he lacks the moody intellectualism of the King of Swords. He's street smart and good at business. He's smart with money.

Is he funny and fun? He isn't the Golden God the King of Wands represents, but he is the man you want to hug and flirt with gently. He knows interesting things and has old school skills.

Is he a great lover? He isn't a virtuoso lover poet like the King of Cups, but he is tender and thoughtful and cares about your pleasure.

He is in all things and all ways a Good Catch, for sure. Devoted, reliable, steadfast, and honest.

You could do worse.

I mean, you could do WAY worse, than this big handsome sweetie.

In his least interesting aspects, he might be a bit dull and lacking in spontaneity, or maybe lacking the creative or intellectual curiosity you might think you need to be utterly fulfilled. Maybe. I tend to want to say here that you should never rely on one person to be all things for you, and this is a good guy. Hang out with friends for that variety, but come home to comfort and love.

This is definitely NOT "settling."

POSSIBLE OUTCOME

Oh yum. Take this opportunity and enjoy yourself. He's the marrying kind.

SOME USEFUL SPREADS

There are many richly detailed books about nothing but Tarot spreads, and that's extremely interesting and loads of fun and I suggest that when you become more expert, these new spreads can be a great tool to use to expand your capabilities.

Still, I find that you need to "trust" your spread for it to accurately tell you what you want to know. By this I mean it's become a good friend; you know each placement by heart, it feels natural to you, and you have used them over time. This is why I use only a few different spreads in my own readings. Classics, as it were, though modified over time.

There are many fancy spreads out there, and if you find one during your travels that resonates with you strongly, USE IT! There is a reason it resonates for you, and you should run with that. But, if you are new to Tarot, try a few classics first, and get to know them well, and you can learn much.

Here are the spreads I use most often, and a sample reading will follow to show the cards in action!

For all readings, I prepare the cards by having the Querent shuffle the deck in ANY way that works for them: traditional card shuffle, smear them into a big pile and then gather them up again, drop them from a really high place and …ok, no. Not that.

Mix them up until they feel "done" in any way you like. You will know when this happens if you keep a calm and focused mind. Don't chat about your day while shuffling; be in the moment, and mix up the cards completely. Then, cut the deck once, re-stack, and draw from the top of the cut.

While doing this, think the following:

"What do I most need to know about ___________?" … filling that blank spot with the subject of interest.

"What do I most need to know about ______'s feelings for me?"

“What do I most need to know about my current relationship's potential?”

“What do I most need to know about that weird behavior ______ engaged in last Saturday?

Keep it simple, keep your mind open, and Tarot will give you more information than you might receive had you thought something very layered...or very specific.

Tarot can often give you very sophisticated answers to very simple questions. Consider handing over the reins and seeing what happens!

ISSUE-ACTION-OUTCOME

This is a variation on the classic three card Tarot spread of "Past-Present-Future", and I find it to be much more useful!

Shuffle the cards till they are done while focusing on your area of interest. Cut the deck once and draw from the top of the cut.

Lay three cards out, from left to right.

Turn them over (again, I read only upright, as the deck is already perfectly balanced, but it can be helpful to notice when a card is reversed, as it can mean a less vibrant expression of its meaning).

Here is a sample reading of three cards. This was a spread that a friend got in response to a question regarding a man she was dating who had suddenly started pulling away:

1. Issue: Two of Swords

2. Action: Hanged Man

3. Outcome: Temperance

This is rich with information, in spite of being only three cards, so let's unpack this first and fundamentally useful spread carefully.

The Issue: Two of Swords.
Stalemate. Impasse. Rejection of love offered, emotional withdrawal. The Love Avoidant attachment style. Good times here. Could mean you dig Spock, but usually it means something once embraced is currently being rejected. Painful.

Action: Hanged Man

As we know from reading the definitions of the cards, the Hanged Man is a strong admonition to take your hands OFF a situation, and realize the less you do, the better the result. Things are happening to you and around you, and yes, it feels like you're twisting in the wind, but this is a case where it is a fertile time of withholding in order to be able to express yourself later.

This card strongly says "Do nothing. Back off. You have no control here."

Outcome: Temperance

Peace. Balance. Calm, and contentment. Not a card of boredom. A card of healing. Especially good if Querent is in a state of ill health or stress currently, as it suggests freedom and healing.

So there is a rather obvious interpretation here, and that is that her new man is definitely withdrawing, she most definitely feels helpless, and it is painful. Doing anything, chasing after him, anything at all, will make it worse. It ALSO suggests that if she refrains from doing this, the result is that he will return, and calm will reign.

Sounds nice on the surface, and it is, for a while, but let's look deeper.

I would expand on this. People tend to assume that they can engage in a behavior indefinitely. That they can just "Be more quiet", or, "ask for nothing", or somehow hold themselves to a different standard of behavior in order to create a persona that will be pleasing to another...forever.

You can't. You simply cannot do this. Eventually the resentment will reach a fever pitch and you will explode. With an emotionally avoidant or unavailable person, making yourself smaller and smaller in order to not seem needy isn't going to work long term.

A lot of reasonable needs are chalked up to neediness in a world that values detached "chill" more than earnest and sincere desire. You get to have needs. Being discerning as to what is a reasonable need and what is true "neediness" is a muscle you can build up easily, but it takes self-compassion, and a realization that you deserve excellent treatment from the people in your life.

So my friend could ask for less. Need less from this cool person. And as a result, she will get to keep him for a while. But at what cost?

He is near her, they might get naked together regularly, but her needs for deeper connection remain unfulfilled.

When reading Tarot, looking deeper can show you how issues of fit are fundamental here. These are two people with different basic needs. They both can change behavior but the needs are still there and will not change. Stalemate might be achieved, and it IS possible that if she asks for next to nothing this skittish unicorn of a man might actually calm down and let her pet him and make him hers; it DOES happen...but you are rarely the exception to the rule; it's why they are called exceptions.

BUT...

Here's an important caveat: Am I reading a lot into a little spread? POSSIBLY.

I'm doing this because this is the easiest and most useful go-to spread around, and I want to show you how much you can get from so little.

Still…

Sometimes a spread like this means simply that the man in question is having a bad week, and if you back off, all will be well. That is why it is important to look at the whole spectrum of outcomes, and then gently hold both in your minds eye. On one hand, it could just be a bad week, on the other hand, this guy could be an emotionally unavailable six month time-suck that you would be better off dumping as soon as you know for sure that this is going to be a permanent state.

So WHAT TO DO? Well, you have been given advice. Do little, back off, and observe, in this instance. There are plenty of cards that will tell you to DO SOMETHING, but not in this case. Now is the time to pay attention. So, no action for a while. Set a timetable. A week, let's say. The situation will provide you with answers if you pay attention. Does he come back warm and open and apologetic? Good sign. Let's give it another week!

Does he come back, but is still emotionally reticent, and maybe holding you to a new "reality" where he gets to be less available but you are still expected to be lover and confidant? Hm. Ok. Want another week to confirm it? You know best. Trust your gut, and then act with the love you feel for yourself, which I hope is abundant, Star Pirate. Don't snack on crumbs and call it toast.

There is a happy ending here. The reading let my friend know to pull back, and so she did, and over the course of a month realized that she was dealing with a man who would always run hot and cold. As a result, she stopped twisting herself to fit his needs at the moment, and took care of herself first. The relationship died a quick and natural death, with little pain to her, and left her open to meet the real sweetheart who was open, wanted the same thing in a relationship as she did, and was delighted to express his feelings towards her consistently and openly.

FIVE CARD SPREAD: DEEPER WATERS

This is an extremely useful, but not overly complicated spread that is handy for when you are feeling confused about your own motivations and wanting advice, rather than to simply see the future.

Five cards, left to right, in a simple line:

1. The Crux of the Matter

2. Your Secret Feelings

3. What You Don't Know

4. What You Should Do About It, or be aware of going forward.

5. The Outcome

Here is a delightful real life example of this spread in action that I shall never forget!

The person asking the question was a woman, very much in love, contemplating marriage with a man who was very traditionally masculine. Herself, very liberal, feminist, and free spirited.

The spread suggested she had everything she needed to be very happy with this man (in spite of a lack of obvious fit), and that marriage was their possible destination.

Here are how my client's cards fell:

1. Three of Cups

2. Emperor

3. Empress

4. Strength

5. Four of Wands

Ooh! Good Stuff here!

1.The Crux: Three of Cups: Celebration! Traditionally, a wedding. We are off to an accurate start.

2. Her Secret Feelings: The Emperor. Will his loving but traditionally macho ways grow oppressive over time? Will there be a bait and switch? Will he be loving now, controlling later? The Emperor is a fine man, but what if?

3. What you don't know: The Empress. How delightful it is when these two Uber Monarchs show up in a spread together. It traditionally means not only are you very well suited, but you are a wonderful balancing act for each other...each bringing playfulness and stability as needed. Sexy.

4. What you should do about it: Strength. The Strength card not only suggests that the Emperor is a good-hearted and loving guy in spite of his exterior traditionalism, but that he admires Our Empress's strength and adores her free-spirited soul.

Additionally, she, as the Empress, has everything she needs in the way of emotional intelligence, charm, and strength to handle this larger than life man. They appear to be a match, and that's excellent, because:

5. The Outcome: Four of Wands. Not only does it go well, as well as strongly suggest marriage in a traditional interpretation of this card, but the Four of Wands is about "expected good turning out even better than expected"...in other words. What you hope for is achieved, and THEN SOME.

This is a dream spread, really, and is full of romance. They DID marry, and while I am sure that particular Star Pirate didn't make a life decision based on a Tarot spread (Because that would not be smart, RIGHT?)....I want to think it helped throw a few rose petals on their path.

THE CLASSIC: THE CELTIC CROSS SPREAD

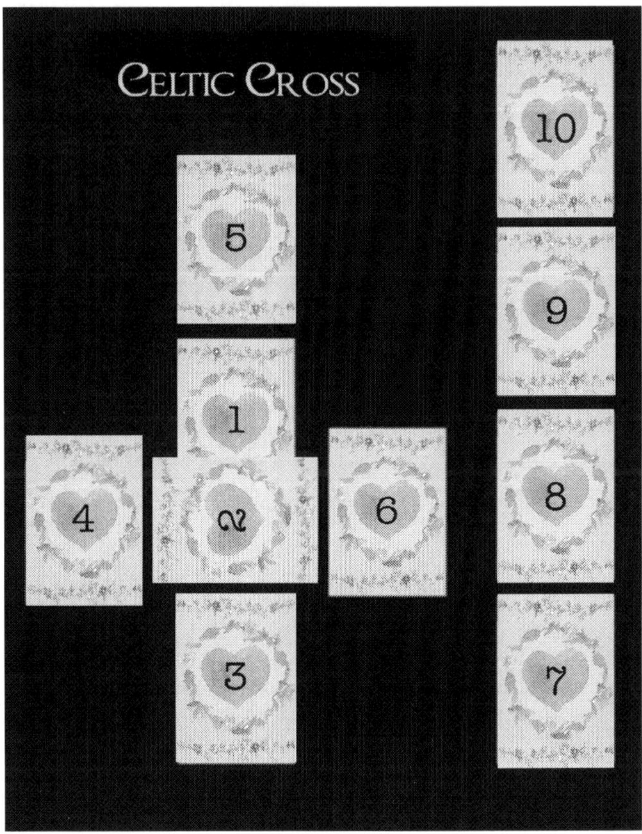

Probably the most famous Tarot spread in the world. So much so that I considered not including it here, but there is a reason it is the most famous spread. It works. And, it has a long, long history of working, so it's very energetically charged, so to speak. I use it regularly.

There are whole books devoted to this spread, so I will do my best to condense a sample reading here to something easily grasped. You don't have to be a master to use it...it's a Giver right out of the box.

Just keep doing it over and over (not the same question, obviously), till you know the card positions backwards and forwards, and then it will start to tell a story, even when not obvious at first glance.

As with all spreads, shuffle and cut as discussed above, while thinking about your query.

There are ten cards, arranged as pictured here. Their placement meanings are:

1. Overview of situation

2. New influences or obstacle that crosses your path

3. The basis of the situation/distant past

4. The recent past/influence that is leaving

5. Influence that is coming/near future

6. More near future (five and six should be combined, really)

7. The atmosphere of the future as it progresses

8. How other people affect you

9. Secret hopes or fears.

10. Final outcome

Here is a spread I did recently for a male client who was considering ending a relationship that had become more roommate-like than loving in expression, and while his girlfriend agreed with him and was even supportive, he felt guilty.

Here are how the cards fell:

1. Overview: Seven of Pentacles.

A pause to evaluate, and wondering if the continued investment in a project is worth it. That's about right, yes? When the first card in a spread matches the question, it is a sign of a good reading to come.

2. The Influence/Obstacle that crosses your path: Eight of Pentacles.

Interesting. This is generally a positive card in a love spread, as it does mean that the people involved want to grow daily, are willing to put in the effort and work to make it happen, and neither takes their partner for granted. Is this a hindrance here, this commitment? More on that in a bit.

3. The Basis: Six of Pentacles.

Lots of earthy, practical Pentacles here!...This says good things about the people involved...both are responsible, generous, stable.. But, it does suggest that this is more practical comfort than love, and the very basis of this relationship is nostalgia and warm association with the past, rather than passion

4. Influence that is leaving: The Moon.

Ah. What was murky under the Moon's influence is going to soon become easier to grasp as it moves to the past. As a result, decisions can be made, perspectives shift, because the whole picture of the relationship, with its troubles as well as triumphs, can be seen. Something needs to change, and soon.

Sometimes it is very hard to call it a day. It is much easier to hang in there, without the stress of change, as evidenced by the obstacle of the Eight of Pentacles in position 2.

Cards 5 and 6, both about the near future, and so I read them as a pair, each equally influencing the other.

Respectively, we have the Eight of Cups, and The Star.

Aw. Bittersweet. Our Querent is feeling a strong desire to walk away from something he has been heavily invested in for years, and he has a lot of hopes and fantasies about what that freedom might look like. Still, so much tenderness between these two. This is most likely a split, but it will not be acrimonious. There is too much love and care here, and neither wants to hurt the other.

Moving further into the future...

Card 7: The Fool. Faith in the Universe to provide. This card suggests that both of the people involved want something to change so badly that they are willing to let go without a plan of

"What's next?". The spread suggests that when they do separate, the positive changes they make in their individual lives will cause a vacuum that will fill up with lovely New People and Experiences. The Fool suggests the Universe is positively itching to get started with this, actually, and that the change is long overdue.

Card 8: How other people influence you: The Four of Swords. Now this is interesting, as in a romance spread this card suggests retreat...solitude, and rest. And this makes sense here, if you think about it.

When you are contemplating ending a relationship, you might have a lot of Big Ideas About Your Fabulous New Life that is just about to start...but in truth, for most of us, there needs to be a period of rest and alone time, to recharge, or heal, and contemplate what you need in a relationship, as it will shift with time and experience.

I'm not of the belief this is needed EVERY time, by the way. Nor do I think every "too soon" new relationship is a rebound, or that you need to wait a set amount of time before you dive back in the pool.

Sometimes, Mr. or Ms. Wonderface just shows up when they show up, least expected and marvelous, and you get to roll with the beautiful surprise of it all.

For most of us mere mortals, though, there will be a few months of Thai takeout and Netflix, and that is ok. It can be wonderful, in fact. So, ultimately, for position 8, and in this case, how "other people influence you" , they are doing so by simply Not Being There. It's you and you for a bit, Star Pirate, and this means you can binge watch whatever you want and don't have to share the green curry. So there.

Card 9: The Hermit. I suppose whenever a relationship ends, and, in spite of the fantasy of being inundated with romantic options as soon as you are out the door, even the most appealing of us can hold a fear that this was their last chance, and that they soon will slip into endless loneliness.

My client's fear was that he would become not the desirable bachelor with a redhead on each arm, but the reclusive, lonely guy playing a whole lot of video games, guiltily enjoying himself but no longer engaged in the world, eating a few too many Hot Pockets, and certainly not getting naked with anyone.

BUT, this is a card in a position about fear, not reality, and I double down on this statement given the outcome card, which is:

10: The Sun

You very, very definitely want the Sun as an outcome card, in any circumstance, period.

The Sun is a glorious outcome card, and in this case very apt. The outcome of ending this relationship...friendly, warm, loving and nurtured as it was, was to shine the light of truth regarding the dissatisfaction with the lack of romance and passion in this otherwise loving couple. The Outcome card takes all the cards that came before it and combines itself with them to let him know that while it won't be an instantly exciting, James Bond like transition to being single again, it will be the right choice. The choice that will lead him to the future happiness projected by the Sun. There is romance in his future, and the Sun is the promise of that. So get some rest, recharge, and get ready to rumble.

So there you have it: A very short history, all the Tarot love interpretations you can eat, and a few useful Tarot spreads to get you into lots of trouble.

I wish you a long and fruitful exploration of these fascinating, endlessly variant and surprisingly subtle cards. They can calm your mind, give you hope, help you think, and sometimes actually tell the future.

I hope you come to love them as much as I do.

Want more? Ok well, thanks! I'm writing another book this very second! How exciting!

You can also get a Tarot reading from me, if you are feeling terribly brave. I am actually very nice, I promise.

If you are interested in having a reading done by me, I offer readings through an Etsy storefront, which you can find here:

www.enlightenedtarot.etsy.com

I also make lovely and unusual Tarot themed jewelry and accessories you can find here:

www.persephonesbijoux.etsy.com

Want to just say hello? Say hi to me on Instagram!

@PersephonesBijoux

Here's wishing you love, Star Pirate.

ACKNOWLEDGEMENTS

Thank you to my wonderful mumma, Pat Stilwell, for her help and unconditional encouragement. She is probably the real reason you are reading this.

Thank you to beautiful and thoughtful Debbie Tune for her help and unfailing support.

Thank you to my friends and clients who helped me be a better reader, encouraged me to write the book, and pestered me lovingly to finish it.

I also very much want to thank again my beautiful Eric, who reminds me daily what it is to be loved truly and well. You are my Sun and Star.

Made in the USA
Monee, IL
05 November 2019

16345214R00083